Best Easy Day Hikes Series

Best Easy Day Hikes
Portland, Oregon

Second Edition

Lizann Dunegan

FALCONGUIDES ®

GUILFORD, CONNECTICUT
HELENA, MONTANA
AN IMPRINT OF THE GLOBE PEQUOT PRESS

FALCONGUIDES®

Copyright © 2009 by Morris Book Publishing, LLC

ALL RIGHTS RESERVED. No part of this book may be reproduced or transmitted in any form by any means, electronic or mechanical, including photocopying and recording, or by any information storage and retrieval system, except as may be expressly permitted in writing from the publisher. Requests for permission should be addressed to The Globe Pequot Press, Attn: Rights and Permissions Department, P.O. Box 480, Guilford, CT 06437.

Falcon and FalconGuides are registered trademarks and Outfit Your Mind is a trademark of Morris Book Publishing, LLC.

Maps © Morris Book Publishing, LLC

Library of Congress Cataloging-in-Publication Data is available on file.

ISBN: 978-0-7627-5109-9

Printed in the United States of America

10 9 8 7 6 5 4 3

Contents

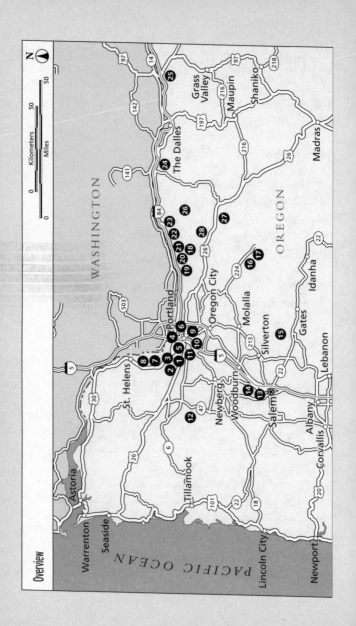

Map Legend

=90=	Interstate
=30=	U.S. Highway
=20=	State Highway
=41=	Local Road
= = = =	Unimproved Road
- - - - -	Trail
————	Paved Trail
■■■■■	Featured Route
⊢—⊢—⊢	Railroad Grade
⌒⌒	River/Creek
.·⌒·.	Intermittent Stream
⊣▭⊢	Tunnel
▭	State Park/Natural Wilderness
▭	National Forest/National Park
⌣	Bridge
▲	Campground
⬗	Gate
❓	Information
🅿	Parking
▲	Peak
🛆	Picnic Area
■	Point of Interest/Other Trailhead
🚻	Restroom
🚌	Shuttle
≡	Steps/Boardwalk
❻	Trailhead
∥	Waterfall
🖼	Viewpoint

Introduction

This small pocket guide contains twenty-eight easy day hikes ranging in length from 0.5 mile to 7.0 miles that allow you to explore Portland and surrounding natural areas within a ninety-minute drive of the city. Portland is nestled at the intersection of the mighty Columbia and Willamette Rivers, the deep forests of the Tualatin Mountain Range, and the diverse landscapes of the Willamette Valley and is just a short drive from magnificent Columbia River Gorge and scenic Mount Hood. This beautiful city is host to a vast system of parks. Many of the parks have interconnected trails that wind through a variety of natural landscapes that nurture your desire to get out and explore. Whether you want to experience an easy stroll along the banks of the Willamette River, enjoy the immense beauty of a natural waterfall in the Columbia River Gorge, or climb to a windswept summit, *Best Easy Day Hikes Portland, Oregon,* showcases the best of this region's recreational treasures.

Weather

Portland and the Willamette Valley receive about 40 inches of rain per year. Expect rain starting in November and lasting through June. All this rain means that trails can be muddy and wet in winter. If you're prepared for these conditions, you'll find that hiking during the winter months means fewer people and more solitude. Hikes located in the eastern part of the Columbia Gorge are typically drier than in Portland and the Willamette Valley, making this area a good place to visit if it's rainy and wet in Portland. You can expect snow on trails above 4,000 feet beginning in late October and sometimes lasting through the end of June. Trails on Mount Hood sometimes do not open until July, depending on the depth of the snowpack. The driest hiking weather in Portland is July through October.

Preparing for Your Hike

Planning your hiking adventure begins with letting a friend or relative know your trip itinerary so that they can call for help if you don't return at your scheduled time. Your next task is to make sure you are outfitted to experience the risks as well as the rewards of the trail. This section highlights clothing and gear you may want to take with you to get the most out of your day hike.

Clothing

Clothing is your armor against Mother Nature's little surprises. Clothing that can be worn in layers is a good strategy for dealing with the often rainy Portland weather. In the spring, fall, and winter months, the first layer you'll want to wear is a wicking layer of long underwear that keeps perspiration away from your skin. Long underwear made from synthetic fibers is an excellent choice. Synthetic fabrics wick moisture away from the skin and draw it toward the next layer of clothing, where it evaporates. Avoid long underwear made of cotton; it is slow to dry and holds moisture next to your skin.

Your second layer should be an insulating layer. In addition to keeping you warm, this layer needs to "breathe" so that you stay dry while hiking. Fleece provides insulation and dries quickly; a zip-up jacket made of this material is highly recommended.

The last line of layering defense is the shell layer. You'll need some type of waterproof, windproof, breathable jacket that will fit over all your other layers. The shell should have a large hood that will fit over a hat. You'll also need a good pair of rain pants made from a similar waterproof, breathable fabric.

Now that you've learned the basics of layering, don't forget to protect your hands and face. In cold, windy, or rainy weather, you'll need a hat made of wool or fleece and insulated, waterproof gloves that will keep your hands warm and toasty. They'll allow you to remove your outer gloves for delicate work without exposing the skin. During the warm summer months, you'll want to wear a wide-brimmed hat, sunglasses, and sunscreen. If you're hiking in spring and summer on a trail next to a lake, creek, or river, be sure to carry mosquito repellent in your pack.

Shoes and Socks

Lightweight hiking boots or trail running shoes are an excellent choice for day hiking. If you'll be hiking in wet weather often, boots or shoes with a Gore-tex liner will help keep your feet dry.

Socks are another important consideration. Steer clear of cotton socks in favor of socks made of wool or a synthetic blend. They provide better cushioning, wick moisture away from your feet, and help prevent blisters.

It's always a good idea to bring an extra pair of sandals or an old pair of tennis shoes along if you plan on wading in creeks or swimming in rivers.

Once you've purchased your footwear, be sure to break it in before you hit the trail. New footwear is often stiff and needs to be stretched and molded to your foot.

Backpacks

To make your day hike more enjoyable, you'll need a day pack to carry basic trail essentials. A day pack should have some of the following characteristics: a padded hip belt that's at least 2 inches in diameter (avoid packs with only a small piece of nylon webbing for a hip belt); a chest strap (which helps stabilize the pack against your body); external pockets to carry water and other items that you want easy access to; an internal pocket to hold keys, a knife, a wallet, and other miscellaneous items; an external lashing system to hold a jacket; and a hydration pocket for carrying a system (a water bladder with an attachable drinking hose). Some hikers like to use a fanny pack to carry a camera, food, a compass, a map, and other trail essentials. Many fanny packs have pockets for two water bottles and a padded hip belt.

Day Hiking Checklist

- day pack
- water and water bottles/water hydration system
- food; high-energy snacks
- first-aid kit
- GPS unit or compass and map
- sunscreen and sunglasses
- matches in waterproof container and fire starter
- insulating top and bottom layers (fleece, wool, etc.)
- rain gear
- winter hat and gloves
- wide-brimmed sun hat, sunscreen, and sunglasses
- insect repellent

- backpacker's trowel, toilet paper, and resealable plastic bags
- camera/film-memory card
- cell phone
- guidebook
- watch

Trail Regulations/Restrictions

Trails in this guide are located in city parks, state parks, national scenic areas, national forests, wildlife refuges, and Bureau of Land Management (BLM) lands. Trails located in city parks do not require special permits or charge use fees.

Trailhead fees at some national forest and national scenic area trailheads require a Northwest Forest Pass. You can buy a day pass or an annual pass. For participating national forests and locations for purchasing a Northwest Forest Pass, call (800) 270-7504 or go online to www.fs.fed.us/r6/passespermits.

A majority of Oregon's state parks require a day-use permit, or you can purchase an annual state park permit. You can purchase passes at self-pay machines located at state park trailheads and visitor centers. To purchase an annual state park pass, call (800) 551-6949 (credit card orders only) or visit www.oregon.gov/OPRD/PARKS/index.shtml.

Choosing a Hike

Although all the hikes in this book are relatively easy, some are longer and have more elevation change than others. To help you pick the type of hike you want, the at-a-glance information at the beginning of each hike includes a short description, the hike distance in miles and type of trail (loop or out and back), the time required for an average hiker, the approximate elevation gain, the best season for hiking the trail, other trail users, whether dogs are allowed on the hike, applicable fees or permits, maps, a trail contact for additional information, and instructions for finding the trailhead.

Maps

The hikes in this book are easy to follow. The maps provided show each trail, so you won't need to buy extra maps. If you decide to explore farther or go off-trail, however, you'll need more detailed maps. All the hikes in this book are covered by the detailed topographic maps published by the U.S. Geological Survey (USGS)—available through local outdoors shops or by calling (888) ASK-USGS or visiting http://store.usgs.gov—and by Maptech CD. If a park trail map is available, that source is also listed.

Zero Impact

The trails in the Portland area are quite popular and sometimes can take a beating. Because of their popularity, we, as trail users and advocates, must be especially vigilant to make sure our passing leaves no lasting mark.

These trails can accommodate plenty of human travel if everyone treats them with respect. Just a few thoughtless, badly mannered, or uninformed visitors can ruin them for everyone who follows. The book *Leave No Trace* is a valuable resource for learning more about these principles.

Three Falcon Zero-Impact Principles

- Leave with everything you brought.
- Leave no sign of your visit.
- Leave the landscape as you found it.

Most of us know better than to litter. It is unsightly, polluting, and potentially dangerous to wildlife. Be sure you leave nothing behind, regardless of how small it is. Pack out all of your own trash, including biodegradable items like orange peels, which might be sought out by area critters. You might also pick up any trash that others have left behind.

Follow the main trail. Avoid cutting switchbacks and walking on vegetation beside the trail. Select durable surfaces, such as rocks, logs, or sandy areas, for resting spots.

Don't pick up souvenirs, such as rocks, shells, feathers, driftwood, or wildflowers. Removing these items will only take away from the next hiker's experience.

Avoid making loud noises that may disturb others. Remember, sound travels easily along ridges and through canyons.

Finally, remember to abide by the golden rule of backcountry travel: If you pack it in, pack it out! Thousands of people coming behind you are thankful for your courtesy and good sense.

Trail Finder

Best Hikes for Waterfalls
- Silver Falls State Park
- Latourell Falls
- Bridal Veil Falls
- Elowah Falls–Upper McCord Creek Falls
- Wahclella Falls
- Eagle Creek

Best Hikes for Geology Lovers
- Mount Tabor
- Powell Butte
- Larch Mountain Crater–Sherrard Point

Best Hikes for Children
- Hoyt Arboretum Loop
- Eastbank Esplanade–Tom McCall Waterfront Park Loop
- Mount Tabor Park
- Powell Butte Park
- Tryon Creek State Park
- Hagg Lake
- Minto–Brown Island Park
- Willamette Mission State Park
- Larch Mountain Crater–Sherrard Point
- Wahclella Falls
- Historic Columbia River Highway State Trail
- Deschutes River State Park Trail
- Lost Lake Loop
- Mirror Lake Loop

Best Hikes for Dogs
- Hoyt Arboretum Loop
- Lower Macleay Park to Pittock Mansion
- Wild Cherry–Alder Loop
- Eastbank Esplanade–Tom McCall Waterfront Park Loop
- Marquam Nature Park to Council Crest
- Oaks Bottom Wildlife Refuge
- Warrior Rock Lighthouse
- Mount Tabor Park
- Powell Butte Park
- Tryon Creek State Park
- Hagg Lake
- Minto–Brown Island Park
- Willamette Mission State Park
- Riverside Trail
- Historic Columbia River Highway State Trail
- Deschutes River State Park Trail
- Lost Lake Loop
- Mirror Lake Loop
- Salmon River

Best Hikes for Lake Lovers
- Hagg Lake
- Lost Lake Loop
- Mirror Lake Loop

Best Hikes for River Lovers
- Eastbank Esplanade–Tom McCall Waterfront Park Loop
- Oaks Bottom Wildlife Refuge
- Warrior Rock Lighthouse
- Minto–Brown Island Park
- Willamette Mission State Park
- Silver Falls State Park
- Clackamas River Trail
- Riverside Trail

- Latourell Falls
- Bridal Veil Falls
- Elowah Falls–Upper McCord Creek Falls
- Wahclella Falls
- Eagle Creek
- Deschutes River State Park Trail
- Salmon River

Best Hikes with Great Views

- Lower Macleay Park to Pittock Mansion
- Marquam Nature Park to Council Crest
- Mount Tabor Park
- Powell Butte Park
- Larch Mountain Crater–Sherrard Point
- Mirror Lake Loop

1 Hoyt Arboretum Loop

This route travels through the spectacular 187–acre tree museum of Hoyt Arboretum in Southwest Portland. The path winds through a variety of forested ecosystems including oak woodland, redwoods, ponderosa pine forest, and an amazing grove of bamboo.

Distance: 1.8-mile loop (with options)
Approximate hiking time: 1 hour
Elevation gain: 75 feet
Trail surface: Dirt path and paved path
Best season: Year-round
Other trail users: None
Canine compatibility: Leashed dogs permitted
Fees and permits: No fees or permits required
Schedule: Hoyt Arboretum is open 6:00 a.m. to 10:00 p.m. The visitor center is open 9:00 a.m. to 4:00 p.m. Monday through Friday and 9:00 a.m. to 3:00 p.m. on Saturday. It is closed on Sunday and major holidays. The visitor center has restrooms and water.
Maps: USGS: Portland; Maptech CD: Newport/Portland/Mount Hood/The Dalles. *Hoyt Arboretum: A Guide to the Trails and Collections* is available at the visitor center.
Trail contact: Hoyt Arboretum, 4000 Southwest Fairview Boulevard, Portland 97221; (503) 228-8733; www.hoytarboretum .org.

Finding the trailhead: From downtown Portland head 1.8 miles west on U.S. Highway 26 toward Beaverton. Take exit 72 for the Oregon Zoo and the World Forestry Center. At the end of the off-ramp, turn right onto Southwest Knights Boulevard and continue past the zoo parking lot and the Forestry Center to the intersection with Southwest Fairview Boulevard. Turn right onto Southwest Fairview and continue 0.1 mile to the arboretum's visitor center and parking area on the right. *DeLorme: Oregon Atlas & Gazetteer:* Page 66 D3

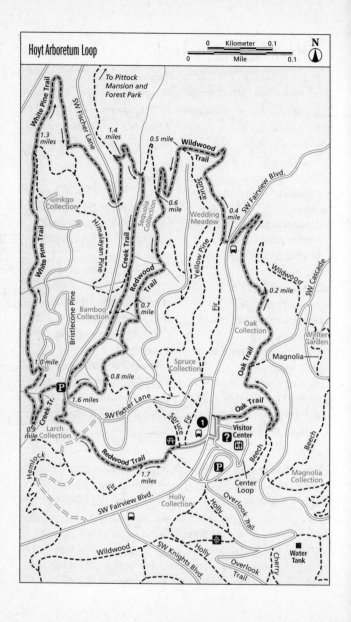

Hoyt Arboretum Loop

To Pittock Mansion and Forest Park

White Pine Trail

SW Fischer Lane

1.3 miles

1.4 miles

0.5 mile

Wildwood Trail

Ginkgo Collection

Himalayan Pine

Sequoia Collection

0.6 mile

Spruce

SW Fairview Blvd.

0.4 mile

Wedding Meadow

Creek Trail

Redwood Trail

0.7 mile

Yellow Pine

Wildwood

0.2 mile

White Pine Trail

Bristlecone Pine

Bamboo Collection

SW Cascade

Oak Collection

Winter Garden

Magnolia

1.0 mile

0.8 mile

Spruce Collection

Oak Trail

Creek Tr.

P

1.6 miles

SW Fischer Lane

Spruce

Fir

0.9 mile

Larch Collection

Oak Trail

1

Visitor Center

?

Beech

Hemlock

Redwood Trail

Fir

1.7 miles

P

Center Loop

Magnolia Collection

Beech

SW Fairview Blvd.

Holly Collection

Overlook Trail

Wildwood

SW Knights Blvd.

Holly

Holly

Overlook Trail

Cherry

Water Tank

The Hike

Hoyt Arboretum was founded in 1928, and the first trees were planted in the 1930s. The arboretum has more than 5,000 labeled plants and trees representing more than 1,000 species. Before you start the hike, be sure to stop at the visitor center. This loop route takes you past several groves of tree species that are grouped by family. You'll start off on the Oak Trail, which takes you through a sunny oak woodland filled with black oak, Japanese evergreen oak, and Konara oak. The path then travels through an immense grove of Russian elm trees and transitions into a stately stand of ponderosa pines with a thick understory of sword fern and vine maple.

After 0.5 mile you'll arrive at an amazing grove of rare dawn redwood trees. Seedlings for this ancient tree were planted here in 1951, and in 1952 the first seed-bearing cones were produced. As you continue, the path switchbacks downhill through a thick grove of giant sequoia trees. At 0.6 mile you'll turn onto the Redwood Trail and walk past a large stand of coast redwood trees, incense cedar, and Port Orford cedars. The trail is also lined in season with twinflower, trillium, and starflower.

After 0.9 mile you'll turn onto the White Pine Trail, which heads uphill past small groves of Swiss stone pine and Korean pine and then transitions to a Douglas fir forest dotted with maidenhair fern, sword fern, and wild raspberries. After 1.4 miles you'll turn onto the Creek Trail, which parallels a small creek and takes you through dense woodland made up of spectacular coast redwoods. The route then travels through an amazing collection of bamboo. Thick bunches of blue fountain bamboo are particularly impressive. At 1.6 miles you'll turn onto the Redwood Trail and follow it back to the visitor center and trailhead. This route is only one of dozens you can explore in Hoyt Arboretum. Use the trail cues below to follow this route, or use the map to make up your own route.

Miles and Directions

0.0 Start by walking on the paved trail next to the visitor center that parallels Southwest Fairview Boulevard. The paved trail ends and joins the signed Oak Trail.

0.1 Turn left and continue descending on the Oak Trail.

0.2 Take a sharp left onto the Wildwood Trail and begin heading uphill. (FYI: The trail winds through a shady grove of Russian elm trees.)

0.4 Cross Southwest Fairview Boulevard and then turn right onto the signed Wildwood Trail.

0.5 The trail intersects the Spruce Trail. Continue straight (right) on the signed Wildwood Trail. (FYI: About 100 yards past the trail junction, be sure to stop and admire the magnificent dawn redwood tree on the left side of the trail. An interpretive marker in front of the tree explains its history.)

0.6 Turn left onto the signed Redwood Trail. At the next trail junction, turn right to stay on the Redwood Trail.

0.7 Continue straight (left) on the Redwood Trail. (A spur trail leading to the Creek Trail heads right.)

0.8 Turn right to stay on the Redwood Trail. At the next trail junction, cross Southwest Fischer Lane and then turn right. Continue a few feet until you reach a parking area. Turn left and walk through the parking area and continue on the signed Creek Trail.

0.9 Turn right onto the signed White Pine Trail. (The Creek Trail continues to the left.)

1.0 Veer sharply to the left and continue on the White Pine Trail. The route rambles beneath a shady Douglas fir canopy dotted with wildflowers and wild raspberries. Ignore the spur trail that heads right toward the Bristlecone Pine Trail.

1.2 Cross a singletrack trail and continue straight on the White Pine Trail. Go about 15 yards to another junction with the Himalayan Pine Trail. Continue straight (left) on the White Pine Trail.

1.3 Turn left on the White Pine Trail. (The signed Himalayan Pine Trail heads right.) The trail begins descending and then intersects Southwest Fischer Lane. Cross Southwest Fischer Lane and continue on the White Pine Trail.

1.4 At the T-junction turn right onto the signed Wildwood Trail. The trail heads downhill on a series of short switchbacks. After crossing the creek you'll arrive at a T-intersection. Turn right onto the signed Creek Trail. (The Wildwood Trail heads left.) The route heads up a creek canyon lined with spectacular coast redwood trees.

1.5 Turn left and continue on the Creek Trail. At the next trail junction, continue straight (right) on the Creek Trail. (The trail heading left crosses the creek and is signed TO REDWOOD TRAIL.)

1.6 The trail intersects Southwest Fischer Lane. Turn left and walk about 20 feet along the road's edge. Cross the road and continue hiking on the signed Redwood Trail.

1.7 Continue straight (left) on the Redwood Trail. (The Fir Trail joins the Redwood Trail from the left.) In a short distance the trail passes a picnic shelter on the left. Just after the shelter, continue straight on the paved path that intersects Southwest Fairview Boulevard. Cross Southwest Fairview Boulevard.

1.8 Arrive back at the visitor center and trailhead.

2 Lower Macleay Park to Pittock Mansion

This hilly forest escape begins at Lower Macleay Park and takes you through beautiful Balch Creek Canyon and then heads steeply uphill through deep forest to historic Pittock Mansion. From the mansion's rear lawn you'll have a commanding view of Mount St. Helens, Mount Hood, and downtown Portland.

Distance: 3.8 miles out and back

Approximate hiking time: 2 to 3 hours

Elevation gain: 850 feet

Trail surface: Dirt path, paved path

Best season: Year-round

Other trail users: Joggers

Canine compatibility: Leashed dogs permitted

Fees and permits: No fees or permits required

Schedule: Dawn to dusk

Maps: USGS: Portland; Maptech CD: Newport/Portland/Mount Hood/The Dalles

Trail contact: Portland Parks and Recreation, 1120 Southwest Fifth Avenue, Suite 1302, Portland 97204; (503) 823-7529; www .portlandparks.org

Finding the trailhead: From Interstate 405 north in downtown Portland, take exit 3 for U.S. Highway 30 West/St. Helens. At the end of the off-ramp, stay in the right lane, which turns onto Northwest Vaughn Street, and go 0.6 mile. Turn left onto Northwest 28th Street and travel 1 block. Turn right onto Northwest Upshur Street and proceed 0.2 mile to a parking area at the road's end at Lower Macleay Park. *DeLorme: Oregon Atlas & Gazetteer:* Page 66 D3

The Hike

The route ascends at a moderate pace along bubbling Balch Creek, which is lined with the intense greenery of vine

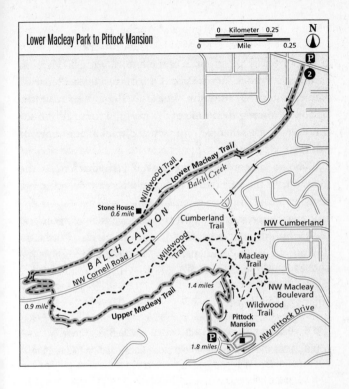

0   Kilometer   0.25

0   Mile   0.25

N

Wildwood Trail

Lower Macleay Trail

Balch Creek

Stone House
0.6 mile

BALCH CANYON

NW Cornell Road

Wildwood Trail

Cumberland Trail

NW Cumberland

Macleay Trail

NW Macleay Boulevard

Wildwood Trail

NW Pittock Drive

Upper Macleay Trail

1.4 miles

0.9 mile

Pittock Mansion

1.8 miles

maple, maidenhair fern, and wild raspberries. This small stream tumbling down the canyon has many rocky pools and small waterfalls that are haven to native cutthroat trout. You'll also see many signs of streambank restoration where hardworking volunteers have planted red cedars and other native plants. After 0.8 mile you'll arrive at Upper Macleay Park, which has restrooms and a picnic area. At this point you'll walk along a dirt path that skirts the edge of a parking area and then cross Cornell Road. From here the route switchbacks steeply uphill through a deep, impressive forest. On this section of the trail, look for the delicate triangular blooms of trillium in March and April.

After 1.8 miles you'll arrive at a paved parking lot adjacent to the parklike grounds of the historic Pittock Mansion estate and Pittock Acres Park. Oregonian editor Henry L. Pittock built this enormous house in 1914. You have the option of touring the inside of the mansion for a fee. To see the current fee schedule, visit www.pittockmansion.org or call (503) 823-3623.

The route continues on a paved path that circles the mansion. At the start of this path you'll pass a small gift shop, restrooms, and drinking fountains. After walking a short distance past impressive gardens, you'll arrive at a viewpoint on the mansion's rear lawn, where you can gaze at Portland's downtown skyline and majestic Mount Hood. Enjoy the views before retracing your route back to the trailhead.

Miles and Directions

0.0 Begin on the paved path located next to Balch Creek.

0.6 Pass the remnant of an old stone house and an intersection with the Wildwood Trail to the right. Continue straight (left) and continue hiking along the creek.

0.7 Cross the creek over a wood bridge and head up a couple of steep switchbacks.

0.8 Continue walking on the dirt trail as it parallels the parking area at Upper Macleay Park. Cross Northwest Cornell Road (watch for traffic) and pick up the trail on the other side.

0.9 Take a sharp right turn and continue uphill on the Upper Macleay Trail. The trail ascends a few steep switchbacks through a shady Douglas fir forest.

1.4 Take a sharp right turn and begin climbing for another 0.4 mile.

1.8 Arrive at the Pittock Mansion parking lot. Continue on the paved path that heads toward the mansion's rear lawn.

2.0 End the loop around the mansion. Retrace the same route back to the trailhead at Lower Macleay Park.

3.8 Arrive back at the trailhead at Lower Macleay Park.

3 Wild Cherry–Alder Loop

This loop route takes you on a tour through Portland's amazing 5,000-acre Forest Park—one of the largest city parks in North America.

Distance: 4.9-mile loop
Approximate hiking time: 2 to 3 hours
Elevation gain: 450 feet
Trail surface: Dirt path, sidewalk, stairs
Best season: Year-round
Other trail users: Joggers
Canine compatibility: Leashed dogs permitted
Fees and permits: No fees or permits required

Schedule: Dawn to dusk
Maps: USGS: Linnton, Portland; Maptech CD: Newport/Portland/Mount Hood/The Dalles
Trail contact: Portland Parks and Recreation, 1120 Southwest Fifth Avenue, Suite 1302, Portland 97204; (503) 823-7529; www.portlandparks.org

Finding the trailhead: From Interstate 405 north in downtown Portland, take exit 3 for U.S. Highway 30 West/St. Helens. At the end of the off-ramp, stay in the right lane, which turns onto Northwest Vaughn Street. At the first stoplight turn left onto Northwest 23rd Avenue. Go 1 block and turn right onto Northwest Thurman Street. Go 1.4 miles to the end of Northwest Thurman Street and park near the green metal gate. Leif Erikson Drive starts at the green metal gate. *DeLorme: Oregon Atlas & Gazetteer:* Page 66 D3

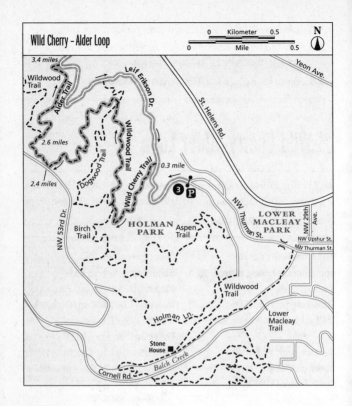

Wild Cherry – Alder Loop

The Hike

This loop route travels beneath the lush canopy of 5,000-acre Forest Park. Thanks should go to those living in Portland at the turn of the twentieth century who had the foresight to secure what today is a wonderful park system enjoyed by hikers, runners, and mountain bikers alike.

Forest Park is part of a forested ridge local Indians called "Tualatin Mountain." As settlements sprang up along the

Willamette River and the west side of Tualatin Mountain in the early 1800s, the original Indian routes over the mountain were improved and expanded. These improvements allowed farmers on the west side of Tualatin Mountain to take advantage of export opportunities and expanding settlements along the Willamette River. This also allowed for extensive logging on the mountain. What was once an evergreen forest of Douglas fir, western hemlock, and western red cedar is now mostly red alder and giant leaf maple.

In the Olmstead report of 1903, John C. Olmstead, a landscape architect from Brookline, Massachusetts, recommended to the Municipal Park Commission of Portland that the woodlands of Tualatin Mountain be purchased for a public park. Unfortunately, between 1915 and 1931 the land became embroiled in shifty real estate schemes. As a result, more than 1,400 acres of residential lots were forfeited to the city of Portland, and additional land on Tualatin Mountain was acquired by Multnomah County due to delinquent taxes. No land was purchased for park use. In 1947 and 1948 Multnomah County and the City of Portland transferred 2,500 acres of this land to the Portland Bureau of Parks. Forest Park was, at last, dedicated in September 1948.

You'll begin this route on Leif Erikson Drive, which winds for 11 miles through the park. At 0.3 mile you'll turn onto Wild Cherry Trail and begin ascending a series of switchbacks through a shady forest canopy to the intersection with Wildwood Trail at 0.9 mile. This gorgeous single-track trail, the best-known trail in the park, is more than 26 miles long. You'll follow Wildwood Trail as it sweeps along the ridgeline through a shady forest of bigleaf maple and Douglas fir trees. Beginning in April, look for the delicate triangular blooms of trillium; the bright orange globes of tiger lily begin blooming in May. During mid-July wild raspberries make a tasty trail treat.

After 2.6 miles of rolling terrain, you'll arrive at the junction with Alder Trail. You'll follow Alder Trail as it descends to Leif Erikson Drive. From here you'll follow popular Leif Erikson Drive back to the trailhead. The singletrack section of this route can be muddy from November through April. During this time of year, you may want to hike on Leif Erikson Drive, which tends to stay drier in winter.

Miles and Directions

0.0 Go around a green gate and start hiking on Leif Erikson Drive. (FYI: A drinking fountain is located on the right side of the trail just after you go through the green gate.)

0.3 Turn left onto the signed Wild Cherry Trail and begin to ascend.

0.9 Turn right onto Wildwood Trail. Go 15 feet to a trail fork. Turn right and continue on Wildwood Trail.

1.5 Cross Dogwood Trail and continue straight on Wildwood Trail. (**Bailout:** Turning right onto Dogwood Trail will take you back to Leif Erikson Drive. Once you reach Leif Erikson Drive, turn right and follow it back to the trailhead.)

2.4 The trail passes Northwest 53rd Drive on your left. Continue your journey on Wildwood Trail.

2.6 Turn right onto Alder Trail and begin descending.

3.4 Turn right onto Leif Erikson Drive.

4.9 Arrive back at the trailhead.

4 Eastbank Esplanade–Tom McCall Waterfront Park Loop

Portland's Eastbank Esplanade is an urban adventure that gives you a different perspective of Portland's vibrant waterfront. This 1.7-mile-long promenade hugs the east bank of the Willamette River, which flows right through the heart of downtown. Located between the historic Hawthorne and Steel Bridges, this riverfront walking and biking path gives you an unobstructed view of Portland's skyline and boasts unique art sculptures that celebrate Portland's history. The Esplanade also ties the east and west sides of the city's waterfront district together with nice pathways that cross the Steel and Hawthorne Bridges. A walkway on the Steel Bridge allows you to cross the river to Tom McCall Waterfront Park, located on the west bank of the Willamette River, where you can tour the Japanese American Historical Plaza and enjoy many scenic views of the Willamette River.

Distance: 3.7-mile loop
Approximate hiking time: 2 to 3 hours
Elevation gain: 75 feet
Trail surface: Paved path and stairs
Best season: Year-round
Other trail users: Cyclists, joggers
Canine compatibility: Leashed dogs permitted

Fees and permits: No fees or permits required
Schedule: Open all hours
Maps: USGS: Portland; Maptech CD: Newport/Portland/Mount Hood/The Dalles
Trail contact: Portland Parks and Recreation, 1120 Southwest Fifth Avenue, Suite 1302, Portland 97204; (503) 823-7529; www.portlandparks.org

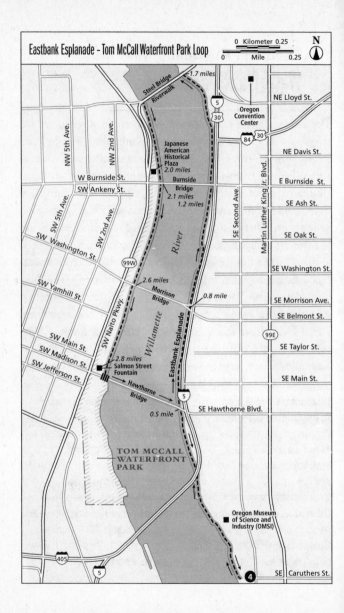

Eastbank Esplanade – Tom McCall Waterfront Park Loop

0 Kilometer 0.25
0 Mile 0.25

N

NE Lloyd St.

Steel Bridge
Riverwalk

1.7 miles

5
30

Oregon
Convention
Center

84 30

NE Davis St.

Japanese
American
Historical
Plaza
2.0 miles

Burnside
Bridge
2.1 miles
1.2 miles

E Burnside St.

SE Ash St.

SE Oak St.

SE Washington St.

River

SE Morrison Ave.

SE Belmont St.

99E

SE Taylor St.

SE Main St.

NW 5th Ave.

NW 2nd Ave.

W Burnside St.

SW Ankeny St.

SW 5th Ave.

SW 2nd Ave.

SW Washington St.

99W

SW Yamhill St.

2.6 miles
Morrison
Bridge

0.8 mile

SE Second Ave.

Martin Luther King Jr. Blvd.

Willamette

Eastbank Esplanade

SW Naito Pkwy.

SW Main St.

SW Madison St.

SW Jefferson St.

2.8 miles
Salmon Street
Fountain

Hawthorne
Bridge

0.5 mile

5

SE Hawthorne Blvd.

TOM MCCALL
WATERFRONT
PARK

405

5

Oregon Museum
of Science and
Industry (OMSI)

4

SE Caruthers St.

Finding the trailhead: From Interstate 5 south in Portland, take exit 300B and get into the left lane. Follow the brown OMSI (Oregon Museum of Science and Industry) signs that take you to Southeast Belmont Avenue, where you'll head east. Turn right (south) onto Seventh Avenue and drive to the intersection with Southeast Clay Street. Turn right (west) onto Southeast Clay Street and drive to the intersection with Southeast Water Avenue. Turn left (south) onto Southeast Water Avenue and proceed to OMSI. Once you reach OMSI continue south on Water Avenue for another 0.3 mile to the intersection with Southeast Caruthers Street. Turn right onto Southeast Caruthers and park on the street where Southeast Caruthers dead-ends at a cul-de-sac.

From Interstate 5 north in Portland, take exit 300, signed for I-84/The Dalles/Portland Airport. Get in the right lane and exit at the OMSI/CENTRAL EASTSIDE INDUSTRIAL DISTRICT sign. Turn right (south) onto Southeast Water Avenue. Proceed 0.7 mile (you'll pass OMSI after 0.4 mile) to the intersection with Southeast Caruthers Street. Turn right onto Southeast Caruthers Street and park on the street where Southeast Caruthers dead-ends at a cul-de-sac. *DeLorme: Oregon Atlas & Gazetteer:* Page 66 D3

The Hike

You'll begin this urban hike by walking north on the Eastbank Esplanade. This wide promenade is lined with attractive benches and native plants and trees. On the first 0.2 mile you'll pass viewing platforms of the river with interpretive signs that tell the story of the endangered chinook salmon, the history of the local Native Americans, and the development of Portland's waterfront.

After 0.8 mile you'll pass under the Morrison Bridge and arrive at a unique bronze sculpture titled *The Echo Gate.* As you continue north, you'll pass *The Ghost Ship,* a lantern made of copperplate, copper bar, stainless steel, and hundreds of prismatic pieces of art glass; *The Stackstalk,* created with steel tubes and a stainless-steel basket suspending a Japanese glass fishing float; and *The Alluvial Wall,* a cold-forged steel plate with bronze castings.

At 1.2 miles you'll turn left and walk down a metal ramp to a 1,200-foot-long floating walkway that takes you to the river's edge. This walkway is 17.5 feet wide and is anchored together with sixty-five concrete pylons—it's the longest floating walkway in the United States. At 1.7 miles stay to the left and cross the Steel Bridge on the pedestrian/bike path. (Periodically this path is closed and you'll have to cross the Steel Bridge on the pedestrian/bike path located on the upper deck.) After crossing the bridge turn left (south) and begin walking along Waterfront Park. The riverside edge of this park is built on top of part of the Portland Harbor Wall. This harbor wall is the most expensive single piece of infrastructure built by the city of Portland. The milelong wall extends from the Steel Bridge to the Hawthorne Bridge and was built as a part of a 1920s urban renewal project. It replaced many of the rotting docks and old pier buildings that once stood here and also introduced the first sewer system on the west side of the river.

At 2.0 miles be sure to take a side trip on the stone path that leads to the Japanese American Historical Plaza, which features large stone sculptures with engravings. After 2.1 miles you'll walk under the Burnside Bridge.

At 2.8 miles you'll pass the Salmon Street Fountain on your right. Complete the loop by crossing the Hawthorne Bridge and turning south back to your starting point.

Miles and Directions

0.0 Start by walking north on the Eastbank Esplanade.

0.1 Pass OMSI on the right.

0.2 Pass viewing platforms with interpretive signs.

0.4 Walk through two chain-link gates and continue walking north on the concrete walk that parallels the river.

0.5 Continue straight. Ignore the concrete path that heads right where a sign indicates HAWTHORNE BOULEVARD EASTBOUND. A short distance past this junction, you'll walk under the Hawthorne Bridge.

0.8 Walk under the Morrison Bridge and pass a bronze sculpture called *The Echo Gate* on your left.

1.2 Turn left at the Southeast Ash Street sign and walk down a metal ramp to a floating walkway.

1.7 Cross the Steel Bridge on the pedestrian/bike walkway. Turn left (south) after crossing the bridge.

2.0 Turn right onto a stone path and then walk through the Japanese American Historical Plaza. After viewing the sculptures, continue walking south on the concrete walk that parallels the river.

2.1 Walk under the Burnside Bridge.

2.4 Pass the entrance to the Portland Sternwheeler on the left.

2.6 Walk under the Morrison Bridge.

2.8 Pass the Salmon Street Fountain on your right. Continue past the fountain, and then head up a set of stairs that take you to the top of the Hawthorne Bridge. At the top of the stairs, turn left and cross the bridge (north side) on the pedestrian/bike path.

2.9 After crossing the bridge, turn left onto a paved path that spirals down to the Eastbank Esplanade.

3.2 At the bottom of the spiral path, intersect the Eastbank Esplanade and turn left (south).

3.7 Arrive back at your starting point.

5 Marquam Nature Park to Council Crest

This trail takes you on a city escape through the fern-filled forest of Marquam Nature Park. You'll follow the single-track trail as it ascends beneath a forested canyon to the 1,073-foot summit of Council Crest. From the grassy lawns at the summit, you'll have spectacular views of downtown Portland and the Cascade volcanoes.

Distance: 3.2 miles out and back

Approximate hiking time: 1.5 to 2 hours

Elevation gain: 745 feet

Trail surface: Dirt path, stairs, paved road

Best season: Year-round

Other trail users: Joggers

Canine compatibility: Leashed dogs permitted

Fees and permits: No fees or permits required

Schedule: Open dawn to dusk

Maps: USGS: Portland; Maptech CD: Newport/Portland/ Mount Hood/The Dalles

Trail contact: Portland Parks and Recreation, 1120 Southwest Fifth Avenue, Suite 1302, Portland 97204; (503) 823-7529; www .portlandparks.org

Finding the trailhead: From Interstate 405 north in downtown Portland, take exit 1B for Fourth Avenue and proceed 0.2 mile north. Turn left onto Southwest College Street. Proceed 1 block and turn left onto Southwest Fifth Avenue. Get in the right lane and travel 0.3 mile. Turn right onto Southwest Caruthers Street. Go 1 block and turn left onto Southwest Sixth Avenue. Travel 0.3 mile to a stoplight at the intersection with Southwest Terwilliger Avenue. Continue straight on Southwest Sam Jackson Park Road (Southwest Sixth Avenue ends here) for 0.2 mile. Just past a large water tower, turn right into the Marquam Shelter parking area. *DeLorme: Oregon Atlas & Gazetteer*: Page 60 A3

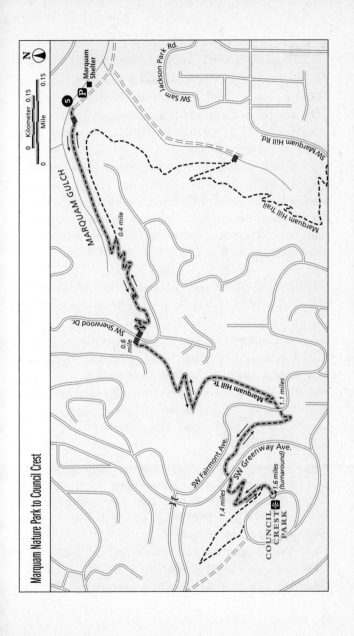

Marquam Nature Park to Council Crest

N

0   Kilometer   0.15

0   Mile   0.15

MARQUAM GULCH

5

P   Marquam Shelter

SW Jackson Park Rd.

SW Sam

SW Marquam Hill Rd.

Marquam Hill Trail

0.4 mile

0.9 mile

SW Sherwood Dr.

Marquam Hill Tr.

1.1 miles

SW Fairmont Ave.

SW Greenway Ave.

1.4 miles

1.6 miles (turnaround)

COUNCIL CREST PARK

The Hike

This hike begins at Marquam Shelter in seventy-one-acre Marquam Nature Park in Southwest Portland. This park is the namesake of Portland pioneer Philip Marquam. The route climbs steeply through a forested canyon filled with bigleaf maple and Douglas fir trees. Raspberries, delicate maidenhair fern, Oregon grape, elderberry, and wildflowers line the trail. Squirrels scamper and chatter in the trees, and songbirds add their own melodies. Look for the thick yellow bodies of banana slugs exploring the moist reserves of fallen trees. While you may think you are all alone in this nature reserve, you'll pass a few large West Hills homes that are tucked away in this quiet green space.

After a steep 1.5-mile ascent, you'll exit the forest canopy and arrive at the spectacular 1,073-foot summit of Council Crest and Council Crest Park. Sweeping views of downtown Portland, Mount Hood, Mount Adams, Mount St. Helens, and Mount Rainier are your reward for all your hard work to reach the summit. Drinking fountains at the summit provide welcome refreshment before you head back to the trailhead on the same route.

Miles and Directions

0.0 Start hiking uphill on an old roadbed that heads right from the Marquam Shelter and is signed COUNCIL CREST. After about 100 yards walk through a metal gate. After the gate, the trail becomes a dirt singletrack.

0.1 Walk up a short set of stairs.

0.4 Take a sharp right at a switchback signed COUNCIL CREST.

0.5 Turn left at a signed intersection.

0.6 Walk up a set of wood stairs. Cross Southwest Sherwood

Drive and hook up with a dirt path that is signed COUNCIL CREST. Continue your uphill trek as the trail crosses a small creek and continues to switchback up the canyon.

1.1 Cross Southwest Fairmont Avenue. Continue walking on the dirt path on the other side, where a sign indicates that you are 0.5 mile from the summit.

1.4 Cross Southwest Greenway Avenue and continue ascending on a dirt trail on the other side.

1.5 Turn left and exit the forest; head another 0.1 mile across a grassy lawn to the summit of Council Crest.

1.6 Arrive at the inviting grassy summit and a stone-wall monument. Soak in the gorgeous views of the Portland metro area and distant mountain peaks, and quench your thirst at the drinking fountains. After taking a break, retrace your route back to the trailhead.

3.2 Arrive back at the Marquam Shelter.

6 Oaks Bottom Wildlife Refuge

This route passes through the expanse of Oaks Bottom Wildlife Refuge in Southeast Portland and is filled with a variety of bird life, including blue herons, Canada geese, and mallard ducks. You may also see beaver, muskrat, and nutria. Black cottonwood, dogwood, and elderberry provide welcoming shade as you hike, and huge thickets of blackberries provide a tasty treat in mid- to late August.

Distance: 3.6 miles out and back

Approximate hiking time: 2 to 3 hours

Elevation gain: 30 feet

Trail surface: Dirt path

Best season: Year-round

Other trail users: Joggers

Canine compatibility: Leashed dogs permitted

Fees and permits: No fees or permits required

Schedule: Open 5:00 a.m. to midnight

Maps: USGS: Lake Oswego; Maptech CD: Newport/Portland/Mount Hood/The Dalles

Trail contact: Portland Parks and Recreation, 1120 Southwest Fifth Avenue, Suite 1302, Portland 97204; (503) 823-7529; www .portlandparks.org

Finding the trailhead: Take exit 297 off Interstate 5 south in Portland, and turn south onto Southwest Terwilliger Boulevard. Drive 0.9 mile to the intersection with Southwest Taylors Ferry Road. Turn left onto Southwest Taylors Ferry Road and continue 1 mile to the intersection with Macadam Avenue (Highway 43). Turn right (south) onto Highway 43 and go 0.5 mile to the Sellwood Bridge. Head east across the Sellwood Bridge. After crossing the bridge turn left onto Southeast Seventh Street. Continue approximately 0.5 mile to the parking lot on the left side of the road at Sellwood Park. *DeLorme: Oregon Atlas & Gazetteer:* Page 60 A3

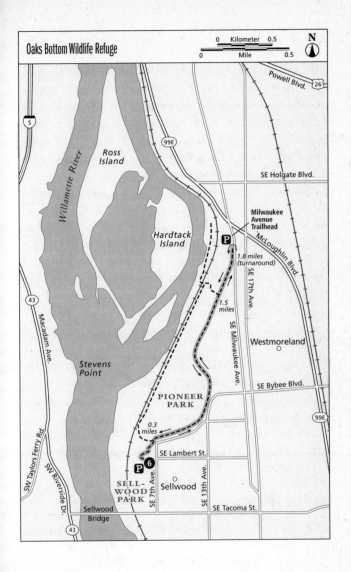

Oaks Bottom Wildlife Refuge

0   Kilometer   0.5

0   Mile   0.5

N

Powell Blvd.   26

Willamette River

Ross Island

99E

SE Holgate Blvd.

Hardtack Island

P

Milwaukee Avenue Trailhead

McLoughlin Blvd.

1.8 miles (turnaround)

SE 17th Ave.

1.5 miles

SE Milwaukee Ave.

Westmoreland

Stevens Point

SE Bybee Blvd.

PIONEER PARK

99E

0.3 miles

SW Taylors Ferry Rd.

SW Riverside Dr.

Macadam Ave.

SE Lambert St.

P   6

SELL-WOOD PARK

Sellwood

SE 7th Ave.

SE 13th Ave.

SE Tacoma St.

Sellwood Bridge

43

The Hike

This route explores 160-acre Oaks Bottom Wildlife Refuge, which was established in 1988 as Portland's first wildlife refuge. The preserve is located on the east bank of the Willamette River in Southeast Portland and is host to more than 140 species of reptiles, birds, amphibians, and mammals. Each winter, thousands of migrating birds feed and rest in the quiet waters of the refuge.

The route begins by heading down a series of switchbacks to a T-junction. You'll turn north and walk along the edge of a large marsh along the banks of the Willamette River. The trail is lined with shady bigleaf maple, Douglas fir, red cedar, black cottonwood, Oregon ash, dogwood, and red osier trees. Be on the lookout for Canada geese, mallard ducks, and great blue herons, which feed in the reeds and rushes of the marsh. Great blue herons are year-round residents and hunt for carp, young salmon, and other fish. They nest on Ross Island from February to June and commute to the refuge to fish. Other wildlife you may see navigating the waters of the marsh are beaver, muskrat, and nutria.

After an easy 1.5-mile stroll next to the marsh, the trail exits the forest canopy adjacent to a large meadow. You'll stay to the right at a trail junction and follow a wide gravel path to the Milwaukee Avenue trailhead and your turn-around point.

Miles and Directions

0.0 Start walking on the dirt path that begins next to the OAKS BOTTOM TRAILHEAD sign. Head down a series of switchbacks past huge thickets of blackberries that ripen in mid- to late August.

0.3 Turn right at an unsigned T-intersection. Continue walking next to the swampy marsh of Oaks Bottom beneath a canopy of black cottonwood, dogwood, and elderberry trees. (FYI: Watch for Canada geese, mallard ducks, and blue herons that feed in the reeds and rushes of the marsh.)

1.5 Arrive at a trail intersection located in an open, grassy meadow scattered with small trees. Turn right and walk up a wide, graveled path to the Milwaukee Avenue trailhead. (**Option:** If you turn left here, you can make a loop. Refer to the trail map.)

1.8 Arrive at the Milwaukee Avenue trailhead. From this trailhead retrace your route back to your starting point at Sellwood Park.

3.6 Arrive back at the trailhead.

7 Oak Island

This peaceful hike takes you through rolling white-oak wood-lands past grassy meadows and fields on Sauvie Island. The trail then travels along the shores of Sturgeon Lake, where you may see blue herons and other abundant bird life.

Distance: 2.9-mile loop
Approximate hiking time: 1 hour
Elevation gain: 15 feet
Trail surface: Dirt path
Best season: Mid-January through the end of September
Other trail users: None
Canine compatibility: Leashed dogs permitted
Fees and permits: Parking permit required; purchase at Sam's Cracker Barrel Store, 15005 Northwest Sauvie Island Road or Reeder Beach RV Park, 26048

Northwest Reeder Road, Portland
Schedule: Open mid-January through the end of September; closed October 1 through mid-January for hunting season
Maps: USGS: Sauvie Island; Maptech CD: Newport/Portland/Mount Hood/The Dalles
Trail contact: Sauvie Island Wildlife Area, 18330 Northwest Sauvie Island Road, Portland 97231; (503) 621-3488; www.dfw.state .or.us/resources/visitors/ sauvie_island_wildlife_area.asp

Finding the trailhead: From Interstate 405 north in Portland, take the U.S. Highway 30/St. Helens exit. Follow signs to US 30 and St. Helens. Follow US 30 for 10 miles north and turn right at the SAUVIE ISLAND WILDLIFE AREA sign. Exit to the right and cross the bridge to the island. After crossing the bridge continue straight on Sauvie Island Road. Continue 2.2 miles and turn right onto Reeder Road. Travel 1.3 miles and then turn left onto Oak Island Road. Go 3 miles to a road fork. Continue straight (the road that goes right heads to a boat ramp) for 0.4 mile to a parking area and the trailhead. *DeLorme: Oregon Atlas & Gazetteer:* Page 66 C2

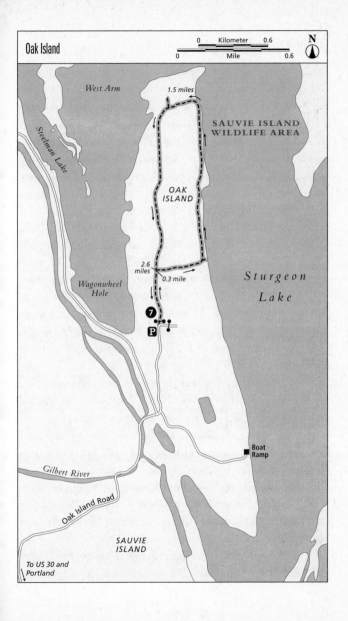

Oak Island

West Arm

Steelman Lake

SAUVIE ISLAND WILDLIFE AREA

1.5 miles

OAK ISLAND

Wagonwheel Hole

2.6 miles

0.3 mile

Sturgeon Lake

7

P

Gilbert River

Oak Island Road

SAUVIE ISLAND

To US 30 and Portland

Boat Ramp

0   Kilometer   0.6

0   Mile   0.6

N

The Hike

At 24,000 acres, Sauvie Island is the largest island in the Columbia River. It is located 10 miles north of Portland off US 30 at the confluence of the Willamette and Columbia Rivers. At 4 miles wide and 15 miles long, the island is characterized by fertile farmland, shallow lakes, sloughs, and groves of cottonwood, oak, willow, and ash. The island is home to more than 300 species of animals, including raccoon, beaver, mink, and black-tailed deer. It is also located on the Pacific Flyway, which attracts thousands of migrating birds each year. The northern half of the island contains a 12,000-acre wildlife area, which is managed by the Oregon Fish and Wildlife Service. During fall, more than 150,000 ducks congregate in the wetlands on the island. You may see mallards, ruddy ducks, green-winged teals, buffleheads, pintails, and widgeons. This rich variety of bird life attracts not only bird-watchers but also hunters. The wildlife area is generally closed October 1 through mid-January for hunting season.

This route explores Oak Island—a small peninsula on the northwest end of Sauvie Island that shoots northward into Sturgeon Lake. This grassy peninsula is covered with thick white-oak woodlands. Small mammals live and feed in the tall wild grasses, and the gnarled branches of the oaks provide shelter for jays, warblers, sparrows, kinglets, chickadees, and nuthatches. Northern harriers sail over the open fields hunting for small mammals, and bald eagles can be seen roosting high in the oak trees from December through March.

You'll begin this route by walking around a metal gate and onto an old roadbed. Be sure to pick up a trail brochure (available in English and Spanish) that explains the history and natural features of the area. The route continues through a thick white-oak woodland. The doubletrack trail is often overgrown with tall grass (it is recommended that you wear long pants on this hike), and blackberries line the trail in a tumbled mass. The delicious, sweet, purplish berries begin to ripen in mid-August. At 0.6 mile you'll arrive at Sturgeon Lake, a haven for geese, ducks, blue herons, swans, and sandhill cranes. A short side trail leads to the edge of the lake, where Mount St. Helens looms in the background. The grassy doubletrack road skirts the edge of the lake for another 0.9 mile. The remaining portion of the loop takes you past grassy fields and oak woodland filled with the chatter of squirrels and songbirds.

Miles and Directions

0.0 Walk around a metal gate and begin walking on a doubletrack road. Pick up a trail brochure at the trailhead sign located on the right side of the road. After a short distance the road forks.

0.3 Turn right and begin the loop portion of the trail.

0.6 Arrive at the edge of Sturgeon Lake. A short side trail leads to a rocky beach by the lake's edge. (FYI: Look for sandhill cranes, blue herons, Canada geese, snow geese, and tundra swans.)

1.5 The grassy track turns left and away from the lake.

2.6 The loop portion of the route ends. Continue straight (right) toward the trailhead.

2.9 Arrive back at the trailhead.

8 Warrior Rock Lighthouse

This route takes you to the tip of Sauvie Island and Warrior Rock Lighthouse. You'll have excellent views of the Columbia River and opportunities to view abundant wildlife.

Distance: 6.0 miles out and back

Approximate hiking time: 2 to 3 hours

Elevation gain: 10 feet

Trail surface: Dirt path

Best season: Year-round

Other trail users: Joggers

Canine compatibility: Leashed dogs permitted

Fees and permits: Parking permit required; purchase at Sam's Cracker Barrel Store, 15005 Northwest Sauvie Island Road or Reeder Beach RV Park, 26048 Northwest Reeder Road, Portland

Schedule: Open all hours

Maps: USGS: St. Helens; Maptech CD: Newport/Portland/ Mount Hood/The Dalles

Trail contact: Sauvie Island Wildlife Area, 18330 Northwest Sauvie Island Road, Portland 97231; (503) 621-3488; www .dfw.state.or.us/resources/ visitors/sauvie_island_ wildlife_area.asp

Finding the trailhead: From Interstate 405 north in Portland, take the U.S. Highway 30 West/St. Helens exit and follow the signs for St. Helens. Travel 9.3 miles north on US 30 until you see a sign indicating Sauvie Island Wildlife Area. Exit to the right and cross the bridge to the island. After crossing the bridge, continue straight (north) on Northwest Sauvie Island Road for 2.3 miles. Turn right onto Northwest Reeder Road and go 13.2 miles until it dead-ends at a gravel parking area (the last 2.2 miles of this road are gravel). *DeLorme: Oregon Atlas & Gazetteer:* Page 66 B2

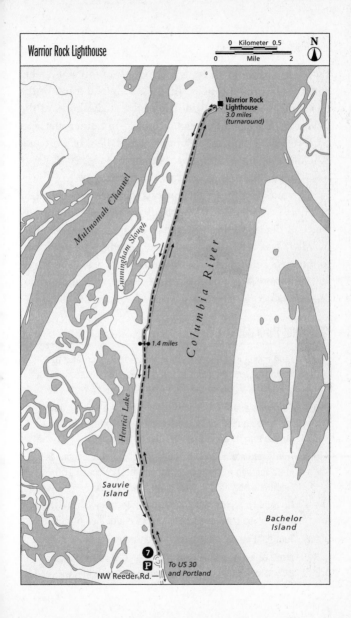

Warrior Rock Lighthouse

0   Kilometer   0.5
0   Mile   2

N

Warrior Rock
Lighthouse
3.0 miles
(turnaround)

Multnomah Channel

Cunningham Slough

Columbia River

1.4 miles

Henrici Lake

Sauvie
Island

Bachelor
Island

7

P

NW Reeder Rd.

To US 30
and Portland

The Hike

Escape from the city to enjoy the solitude of this island hike. The route travels through a thick cottonwood forest to the northern tip of Sauvie Island along the sandy shores of the Columbia River. Large freighters, tugs, and other ships can be seen sailing up the Columbia to the Port of Portland. Wildlife abounds—from great blue herons to bald eagles—not to mention some of the bovine species.

At your halfway point you can view the whitewashed beacon of Warrior Rock Lighthouse, which rests on a sandy beach at the tip of the island. The original lighthouse, built in 1889, was a two-story structure resting on a sandstone foundation and featured a distinctive fog bell. The original lighthouse was replaced in the 1930s with the current 28-foot-tall concrete lighthouse.

Miles and Directions

0.0 Start hiking north on the singletrack trail located next to a wood trail sign adjacent to the parking area. (Note: This section of the route can be a bit wild and overgrown.)

0.4 Step over a low wire fence. As you continue walking down this smooth country lane, keep your eye out for juicy blackberries that begin to ripen in mid- to late August.

0.5 Turn right onto a smooth doubletrack road that continues north through a shady cottonwood forest. Proceed 100 yards and stay to the right at the road junction.

1.4 Go through a blue metal gate. (Note: Be sure to close the gate, or you may let some wily cows out of their pasture.)

2.8 Turn right on the doubletrack road toward the beach.

3.0 Arrive at a long sandy beach. Soak in the views of the expansive Columbia River and whitewashed lighthouse, and then turn around and head back on the same route.

6.0 Arrive back at the trailhead.

9 Mount Tabor Park

Mount Tabor Park is one of those urban sanctuaries where you can still find wild in the city. This prominent volcanic butte rises above Portland's skyline bursting with urban greenery. Where else can you hike to the top of a three-million-year-old volcano covered with a Douglas fir and conifer forest? This 200-acre park is crisscrossed with well-maintained hiking trails, and views from the western summit are stellar. This short route is a good introduction to a beautiful urban park that promises a fun hiking adventure right in the heart of the city. Your canine companion will also enjoy the leash-free dog park located at the south end of the park.

Distance: 2.8-mile loop (with options)
Approximate hiking time: 1 to 1.5 hours
Elevation gain: 250 feet
Trail surface: Dirt path, paved road
Best season: Year-round
Other trail users: Joggers, mountain bikers
Canine compatibility: Leashed dogs permitted
Fees and permits: No fees or permits required

Schedule: Open 5:00 a.m. to midnight; dog park (see map), located on the south side of the park, open 7:00 a.m. to 9:00 p.m.
Maps: USGS: Mount Tabor; Maptech CD: Newport/Portland/Mount Hood/The Dalles; park trail map available online at www.portlandparks.org
Trail contact: Portland Parks and Recreation, 1120 Southwest Fifth Avenue, Suite 1302, Portland 97204; (503) 823-7529; www.portlandparks.org

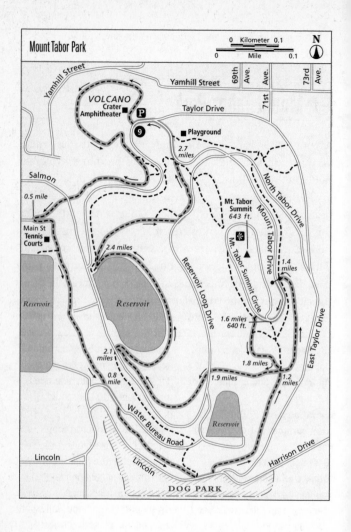

Finding the trailhead: From downtown Portland head 5.5 miles east on Interstate 84 toward The Dalles. Exit the freeway at 82nd Avenue (exit 5). At the end of the off-ramp and stop sign, turn right and go 1 block to a stoplight and the intersection with Northeast 82nd Avenue. Turn left (south) onto Northeast 82nd Avenue and travel 1.1 miles to the intersection with Southeast Yamhill Street. Turn right onto Southeast Yamhill Street and proceed 0.3 mile west to the intersection with Southeast 76th Avenue. Turn right onto Southeast 76th Avenue and then take an immediate left onto Southeast Yamhill Street and continue heading west for 0.3 mile to the intersection with Southeast 69th Avenue. Turn left onto Southeast 69th Avenue; go 1 block and turn right on an unmarked paved road at the base of Mount Tabor Park. Continue 0.2 mile to a parking area on the right side of the road. *DeLorme: Oregon Atlas & Gazetteer:* Page 66 D4

The Hike

Located 4 miles east of downtown Portland, 195-acre Mount Tabor Park has plenty of hiking trails to explore. This park is located on an extinct three-million-year-old volcano, and its 643-foot summit affords stunning views of Portland's east side and peeks of Mount Hood through the trees to the west. Plympton Kelly, an early Portland resident, named Mount Tabor for a mountain located in Palestine. In the early 1900s this park was in a semirural area that was dominated by fruit orchards. Luckily the city recognized this area as a place to preserve. The Parks and Recreation Department began purchasing land for the park in 1909.

Mount Tabor is in the center of Portland's southeast district, and you'll see a wide variety of human-powered crafts cruising the roads and trails in the park. The canine crowd also likes to hang out in the park with their humans in tow.

A large, leash-free dog park—located on the south side of the park—can be enjoyed by your canine companion.

Multiple paths crisscross the butte, making an endless possibility of routes you can explore. The hike described here is a mix of dirt paths and paved roads and gives you a quick tour of the park's highlights. It begins adjacent to the restrooms on a wide, smooth dirt path that travels around the west side of the park through a large grove of Douglas fir trees. It heads downhill past a set of tennis courts and then travels past one of three reservoirs that store drinking water from Bull Run.

After a short uphill jaunt, you'll hike around the east side of the park, where you'll have opportunities to view Mount Hood through the trees. The route then hits the pavement and heads to the summit, where a bronze statue of Harvey W. Scott, former editor of the *Oregonian,* is prominently displayed. Here you'll find many park enthusiasts enjoying the great summit views and soaking up the sun's rays on warm summer days. The hike's grand finale is a quick tour around a smaller butte and then one last downhill jaunt to your starting point. You can check out the hike described here or make up your own route on the park's many trails.

Miles and Directions

0.0 Start hiking on the dirt path that starts in the northeast corner of the parking area next to the restrooms. After a short jaunt, you'll arrive at a trail fork. Turn right and continue through a thick grove of shady Douglas fir trees along the west side of Mount Tabor.

0.3 Cross a gravel road and continue straight on the dirt path.

0.4 Arrive at a four-way junction. Continue straight on the single-track trail. Go 25 yards and arrive at a T-junction. Go right and continue on the singletrack.

0.5 Cross a paved park entrance road and continue straight down the singletrack trail. Go 50 yards and take a sharp left at the drinking fountain; walk parallel to the tennis courts (the courts are on your right).

0.6 Arrive at a trail junction. Stay to the left and crank uphill. You are now above the reservoir. Turn left after crossing a paved path.

0.7 Go right at the trail fork.

0.8 The trail intersects a paved road. Turn left on the paved Water Bureau Road; continue about 50 yards uphill on the road shoulder and then turn right onto a dirt path. Ignore spur trails that head left.

0.9 Turn right onto a dirt path and go about 35 yards. Turn left onto Lincoln, a paved road. (**Option:** If you want to check out the dog park, continue straight across Lincoln to a series of steps that lead downhill into the dog park.) Continue about 50 yards along the road shoulder and then swing a left onto a dirt path. Go 15 yards to a T-intersection. Turn right and crank uphill. At the next trail junction, turn right and continue up the steep grade. Ignore a spur trail that heads to the left.

1.2 Turn right at a five-way junction and continue hiking on the wide dirt path as it goes around the east side of Mount Tabor. (FYI: You'll have sneak peeks of Mount Hood through the trees.) At the next trail junction, turn right and continue on the smooth singletrack trail.

1.4 The trail intersects paved Mount Tabor Drive. Continue straight on Mount Tabor Drive for about 50 yards. Take a very sharp left and go around a white gate; continue walking uphill on the paved summit road.

1.6 Arrive at paved Mount Tabor Summit Circle. Turn left and continue on the paved road.

1.7 Turn left onto a singletrack that heads downhill. Go about 15 yards to a trail junction. Turn right onto a singletrack trail and continue descending. At the next trail junction, veer right.

1.8 Turn right at the five-way junction, and continue descending on the dirt path.

1.9 Cross a paved road, pass a drinking fountain on your left, and turn left onto a dirt singletrack that goes around the base of a small butte.

2.1 Turn right at the trail junction and continue hiking on the singletrack trail. At this point the reservoir is located on the left side of the trail. At the next trail junction, veer left onto a dirt path.

2.2 Enjoy views of Portland's skyline to the west.

2.4 Turn right onto a dirt path that heads up a steep hill. Go about 10 yards to another trail junction. Continue straight (right), and continue cranking up a steep grade.

2.5 Ignore a paved road on your right and continue straight on the singletrack trail. Go a short distance to a junction with another paved road. Turn left onto the paved road.

2.7 Turn left onto a dirt path. Almost immediately the dirt path forks; go right and descend on a singletrack trail. Go about 200 yards, and then turn left onto a paved road opposite a small playground.

2.8 Arrive at a T-junction and stop sign. Turn left onto a paved road, and then take an immediate right into the parking area and your starting point.

10 Powell Butte Nature Park

Powell Butte Nature Park is located on an extinct volcano that features diverse habitats and wildlife. This 570–acre park has more than 9 miles of interconnecting trails that wind through open grassy meadows, old fruit orchards, and thick woodlands made up of western red cedar, Douglas fir, alder, and bigleaf maple trees. This loop trail is a great introduction to the many trails of this scenic nature park.

Distance: 3.5-mile loop (with options)

Approximate hiking time: 1.5 to 2 hours

Elevation gain: 220 feet

Trail surface: Dirt path, paved path

Best season: Year-round

Other trail users: Joggers, mountain bikers, equestrians

Canine compatibility: Leashed dogs permitted

Fees and permits: No fees or permits required

Schedule: Access to the park other than the main parking area is 5:00 a.m. to 10:00 p.m. The parking lot access is restricted to the seasonal hours listed below.

Fall: 7:00 a.m. to 8:00 p.m. (September 1 to the last Saturday in October)
Winter: 7:00 a.m. to 6:00 p.m. (last Sunday in October to the first Saturday in April)
Spring: 7:00 a.m. to 8:00 p.m. (first Sunday in April to May 31)
Summer: 7:00 a.m. to 10:00 p.m. (June 1 to August 31st)

Maps: USGS: Gladstone, Damascus; Maptech CD: Newport/Portland/Mount Hood/The Dalles; park trail map available online at www.portlandparks.org

Trail contact: Portland Parks and Recreation, 1120 Southwest Fifth Avenue, Suite 1302, Portland 97204; (503) 823-7529; www.portlandparks.org

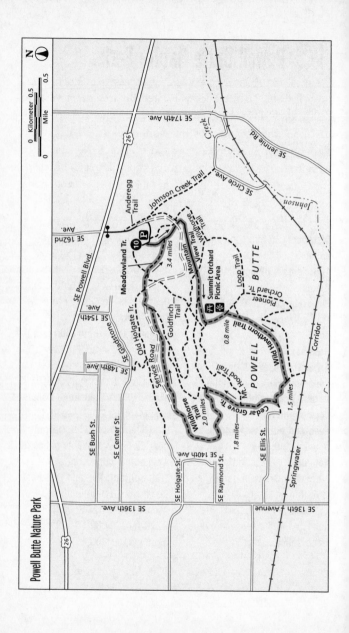

Powell Butte Nature Park

Finding the trailhead: From Interstate 205 in southeast Portland, head east on Southeast Division Street. Go 3.5 miles and turn right onto Southeast 162nd Avenue. Continue 0.7 mile to the entrance of Powell Butte Nature Park. Proceed 0.3 mile to a large parking area and the trailhead. *DeLorme: Oregon Atlas & Gazetteer:* Page 60 A4

The Hike

The city of Portland is full of surprises, and Powell Butte Nature Park is one of the best. This 570-acre park has more than 9 miles of trails for hikers, mountain bikers, and equestrians. Rich in plant and animal diversity, this urban park is characterized by forests of bigleaf maple, Douglas fir, Pacific dogwood, rolling meadows, and an old apple, pear, and walnut orchard. This park is also a wildlife haven where it's common to see birds of prey, black-tailed deer, coyotes, raccoons, and squirrels.

In the early 1900s George Wilson, original owner of Powell Butte, leased the property to Henry Anderegg, who grew crops and raised cattle. In the early 1920s the City of Portland purchased Powell Butte, intending one day to construct a reservoir. In the early 1980s a 500-million-gallon reservoir was finally built and is now part of the Bull Run water system, primary water source for the Portland metropolitan area. Powell Butte Nature Park is part of a larger, interconnected park system in the Portland area, all of which is brought under the Metropolitan Greenspaces Master Plan adopted in 1992. This plan consists of a system of more than 350 miles of trails linking parks, natural areas, open spaces, and greenways.

This loop route is one of many loop combinations you can try in this quiet nature preserve. You'll begin the hike on the paved Mountain View Trail, which ascends at a gentle pace past open grassy meadows. The route then turns onto the Orchard Loop Trail, which winds through an open meadow scattered with groves of black hawthorn and Himalayan blackberry. After 0.8 mile the route turns onto the Wild Hawthorn Trail and descends into a cool forest.

The trail twists and turns through a shady corridor until you arrive at the junction with the Mount Hood Trail. You'll turn onto the Mount Hood Trail and continue as the trail winds past towering red cedar and Douglas fir trees. At 1.8 miles the route continues on the Cedar Grove Trail. Over the next 1.4 miles you'll continue walking beneath a shady forest canopy filled with the pleasant chatter of squirrels and songbirds. Soon you'll exit out of the trees and complete the loop past more wildflower meadows on the Meadowland Trail back to your starting point.

Miles and Directions

0.0 Warm up on the paved Mountain View Trail, which starts on the west end of the concrete patio next to the restrooms.

0.6 Turn right onto the singletrack Orchard Loop Trail. Go another 20 feet and continue straight on the Wildhorse Trail. Continue another 50 feet and turn left.

0.7 Veer left onto the Orchard Loop Trail.

0.8 Turn right onto the signed Wild Hawthorn Trail. The turn for this trail is located 50 feet past the trail sign.

1.5 Turn right at an unsigned dirt intersection. Continue another 100 feet, and then turn right onto the signed Mount Hood Trail.

1.6 Turn right and continue hiking on the Mount Hood Trail.

1.8 Continue straight (left) on the signed Cedar Grove Trail. The trail descends through a maze of green.

2.0 Turn left and cross a small creek. After crossing the creek, head left and continue on the signed Wildhorse Trail.

2.5 Continue straight (right). Ignore the path that drops off steeply on your left.

2.6 Continue straight (left), ignoring the trail on the right that heads steeply uphill. Continue another 30 feet past this intersection and arrive at a crest in the trail. Turn right onto an unsigned dirt trail.

2.8 Turn left onto an unsigned dirt trail.

3.0 Turn right onto a gravel road.

3.2 Veer right where a sign indicates MEADOWLAND TRAIL.

3.4 Continue straight on the Meadowland Trail. After about 200 feet, go left on a singletrack trail that heads downhill toward the restrooms and your starting point.

3.5 Arrive back at the trailhead.

11 Tryon Creek State Park

This 645–acre state park is a forested gem that features more than 14 miles of interconnecting trails designed for hikers, runners, and equestrians. Picturesque Tryon Creek wanders through the heart of this park. Many singletrack trails follow the course of the creek and take you over rolling terrain past immense red cedar, Douglas fir, and bigleaf maple trees. The route described here is only one of dozens of routes you can try.

Distance: 4.0-mile loop
Approximate hiking time: 1.5 to 2 hours
Elevation gain: 440 feet
Trail surface: Dirt path, paved path
Best season: Year-round
Other trail users: Joggers, mountain bikers, equestrians
Canine compatibility: Leashed dogs permitted
Fees and permits: No fees or permits required
Schedule: Park open 7:00 a.m. to 8:00 p.m. daily; nature center open 9:00 a.m. to 5:00 p.m. Monday through Sunday
Maps: USGS: Lake Oswego; Maptech CD: Newport/Portland/Mount Hood/The Dalles; Tryon Creek State Park trail map available at the nature center or online at www.oregonstateparks.org/images/pdf/tryon_map.pdf
Trail contact: Oregon State Parks and Recreation, 725 Summer Street NE, Suite C, Salem 97301; (800) 551-6949; www.oregon.gov/ORPD/PARKS/index.shtml

Finding the trailhead: Take exit 297 off Interstate 5 in Portland, and turn south onto Southwest Terwilliger Boulevard. Continue for 2.7 miles, following signs to Lewis and Clark College and Tryon Creek State Park. Turn right at the Tryon Creek State Park entrance sign. Proceed 0.2 mile on the entrance road to the parking area adjacent to the nature center. *DeLorme: Oregon Atlas & Gazetteer:* Page 60 A3

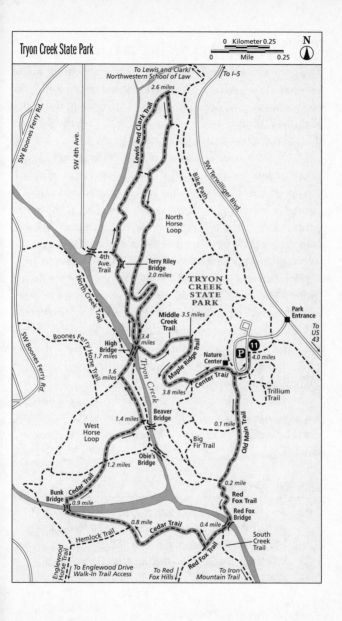

Tryon Creek State Park

0 Kilometer 0.25

0 Mile 0.25

N

To Lewis and Clark/
Northwestern School of Law

To I-5

2.6 miles

SW Boones Ferry Rd.

SW 4th Ave.

Lewis and Clark Trail

SW Terwilliger Blvd.

Bike Path

North Horse Loop

4th Ave. Trail

Terry Riley Bridge
2.0 miles

TRYON CREEK STATE PARK

Park Entrance

To US 43

North Creek Trail

Boones Ferry Horse Trail

SW Boones Ferry Rd.

High Bridge
1.7 miles

1.6 miles

3.4 miles

Tryon Creek

Middle Creek Trail 3.5 miles

Maple Ridge Trail

Nature Center

P

11

4.0 miles

Center Trail

Trillium Trail

3.8 miles

West Horse Loop

1.4 miles

Beaver Bridge

Big Fir Trail

0.1 mile

Old Main Trail

Obie's Bridge

1.2 miles

Cedar Trail

0.2 mile

Bunk Bridge

0.9 mile

0.8 mile

Cedar Trail

0.4 mile

Red Fox Trail

Red Fox Bridge

South Creek Trail

Hemlock Trail

Englewood Horse Trail

To Englewood Drive
Walk-In Trail Access

To Red Fox Hills

Red Fox Trail

To Iron Mountain Trail

The Hike

This route combines several different trails in beautiful 645-acre Tryon Creek State Park. Before you begin your hike, you can pick up a trail map and learn about the park's plants and animals at the nature center. The nature center also has restrooms and drinking fountains.

A large section of the route follows bubbling Tryon Creek as it flows through a shallow forested canyon before it empties into the Willamette River. The route meanders through a second-growth red cedar, Douglas fir, and western hemlock forest and crosses the creek at many different points. Sprinkled into the mix are red alder, black cottonwood, bigleaf maple, and Oregon ash trees.

The different paths wind through a maze of green dotted with yellow violets, trillium, wild ginger, and the feathery fans of sword fern. Yellow-orange-colored salmonberries and wild red raspberries make a tasty trail treat in midsummer. At different points along the path, you'll share the trail with equestrians. If you encounter horses, quietly step off the trail and let them pass.

As you hike, listen for the distinctive calls of blue jays and the chatter of squirrels. Raccoons, skunks, opossums, and black-tailed deer are also residents of this forested park.

Miles and Directions

0.0 Start hiking on the paved path marked TRILLIUM TRAIL, located on the left side of the nature center. Walk 50 feet and then head south on the signed Old Main Trail.

0.1 Veer left on the Old Main Trail. (Note: Big Fir Trail heads right.)

0.2   Turn left onto the signed Red Fox Trail.

0.4   Cross Red Fox Bridge over Tryon Creek, and ascend a series of switchbacks out of the creek canyon. (FYI: Salmonberries and red raspberries provide a sweet treat in midsummer.) At the next trail junction stay to the right on the Red Fox Trail. At the next trail junction, turn right onto the signed Cedar Trail.

0.8   Turn right and continue on Cedar Trail. (Note: Hemlock Trail goes left.)

0.9   Cross Bunk Bridge over rambling Tryon Creek.

1.2   Continue straight on the Cedar Trail.

1.4   Turn left where a sign states WEST HORSE LOOP/HIGH BRIDGE. After 100 yards, continue straight on the main trail, ignoring the unsigned dirt trail that heads right.

1.6   Turn right at a WEST HORSE LOOP/HIGH BRIDGE sign. (The trail going left is signed BOONES FERRY ROAD/ENGLEWOOD DRIVE.)

1.7   Cross High Bridge over Tryon Creek. After crossing the bridge, continue straight. At the next trail intersection, turn left at the LEWIS AND CLARK HIKING TRAIL/LAW SCHOOL sign.

2.0   Cross the Terry Riley Suspension Bridge. After crossing the bridge turn right and continue on the Lewis and Clark Trail.

2.6   Turn right onto an unsigned trail. (The signed Lewis and Clark Trail continues to the left.) Continue about 20 yards to a T-intersection. Turn right toward High Bridge.

3.4   Turn right where a sign indicates HIGH BRIDGE. At the next trail intersection, turn left onto Middle Creek Trail.

3.5   Turn right onto the signed Maple Ridge Trail.

3.8   Turn left onto the signed Center Trail. After this junction, follow signs back to the nature center and your starting point.

4.0   Arrive back at the nature center and trailhead.

12 Hagg Lake

The Hagg Lake Trail passes through open meadows and oak woodlands next to the shores of 1,113-acre Hagg Lake. Rewards along the way include prime blackberry picking, awesome swimming holes, and opportunities to view a variety of wildlife, including deer, coyotes, bobcats, osprey, hawks, bald eagles, songbirds, and a variety of waterfowl.

Distance: 14.1-mile loop
Approximate hiking time: 30 minutes to 5 hours (depending on the length of the hike)
Elevation gain: Varies depending on the trail selected
Trail surface: Dirt path, paved path, paved road
Best season: First weekend in March through mid-November
Other trail users: Joggers, mountain bikers, equestrians
Canine compatibility: Leashed dogs permitted
Fees and permits: Day-use fee March through November

Schedule: Park open dawn to dusk from the first weekend in March through mid-November
Maps: USGS: Gaston, Gales Creek; Maptech CD: Newport/Portland/Mount Hood/The Dalles; Hagg Lake trail map available online at www.co .washington.or.us/deptmts/ sup_serv/fac_mgt/parks/ haggmap.htm
Trail contact: Hagg Lake, 50250 Southwest Scoggins Valley Road, Gaston 97119; (503) 359-5732; www.co.washington .or.us/deptmts/sup_serv/fac _mgt/parks/haggmap.htm

Finding the trailhead: From Portland head 21 miles west on U.S. Highway 26 to the junction with Highway 6. Turn left onto Highway 6 (toward Banks, Forest Grove, and Tillamook) and go 2.5 miles to the intersection with Highway 47. Turn south and proceed 12.5 miles to the junction with Scoggins Valley Road. Turn right (west) onto Scog-

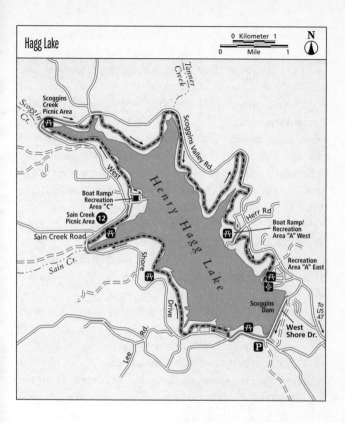

gins Valley Road and head 3.1 miles to the Henry Hagg Lake/Scoggins Valley Park entrance. Go 0.3 mile past the entrance booth to the junction with West Shore Drive. Turn left onto West Shore Drive and travel 3.9 miles to the Sain Creek Picnic Area on the right. *DeLorme: Oregon Atlas & Gazetteer:* Page 59 A7

The Hike

The 14.1-mile Hagg Lake Trail is a wonderful hiking

opportunity close to Portland. This singletrack trail parallels the contours of Henry Hagg Lake and has a variety of terrain: open meadows, forest, stream crossings, bridges, rolling hills, and scenic picnic areas.

Located about 40 miles from downtown Portland, Henry Hagg Lake and Scoggins Valley Park is a popular recreational spot for Tualatin Valley residents. The lake and park are maintained and operated by Washington County and owned by the U.S. Bureau of Reclamation. With 1,113 acres of surface area, the lake was constructed in the mid-1970s to provide supplemental water and flood control for the Tualatin Valley. The lake was named for Henry Hagg, a local dairy farmer who was one of the first people to suggest the reservoir project to the Bureau of Reclamation in 1959. Henry Hagg was a member of the Tualatin Valley Irrigation District, the Agricultural Committee of the Portland Chamber of Commerce, and the Oregon State University Research Committee. He passed away in 1979, four years before the completion of the lake project.

This route begins at Sain Creek Picnic Area, which is equipped with restrooms and a shady picnic area. From the picnic area you can hike in either direction on the lake trail that leads you through open meadows and shady forest, with many viewpoints of the lake. Be aware that sections of this trail may be closed during winter months due to muddy conditions.

Hikers aren't the only persons enjoying this popular park. Boaters, water-skiers, and fishermen also use the lake. The east end of the lake, where there is no wake limit, is used by motorboaters and water-skiers; the west end is reserved for canoeing, sailing, and kayaking.

Miles and Directions

From the Sain Creek Picnic Area, you can hike in either direction on the 14.1-mile Lake Trail.

13 Minto-Brown Island Park

This easy loop explores Minto–Brown Island Park in Salem. The route features views of the Willamette River, cool shady forest, open sunny pastures, and opportunities to view amazing bird life.

Distance: 5.8-mile loop (with options)

Approximate hiking time: 2 to 2.5 hours

Elevation gain: 5 feet

Trail surface: Dirt path, paved path

Best season: Year-round

Other trail users: Joggers, cyclists

Canine compatibility: Leashed dogs permitted; off-leash dogs permitted in designated leash-free area in the park (see map)

Fees and permits: No fees or permits required

Schedule: Open 5:00 a.m. to midnight

Maps: USGS: Salem West; Maptech CD: Newport/Portland/Mount Hood/The Dalles

Trail contact: Salem Parks Operations Division, 1460 20th Street SE, Building #14, Salem 97301; (503) 588-6336; www.cityof salem.net/export/departments/parks/minto_brown.htm

Finding the trailhead: From Interstate 5 in south Salem, take exit 252 (Kuebler Boulevard). Turn west onto Kuebler Boulevard and travel 2 miles. Turn right (north) onto Commercial Street and continue north for 3.5 miles (after 3 miles Commercial becomes Liberty Street). Turn left onto Bush Street. Go 1 block and then turn left onto

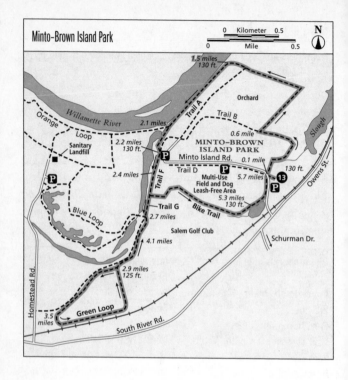

Minto-Brown Island Park

Commercial Street heading south. Proceed to the next light and turn right onto Owens Street. Go 1.2 miles on Owens Street (which becomes River Road), and then turn right onto Minto Island Road. Go 0.2 mile and turn right into a paved parking area and the trailhead. *DeLorme: Oregon Atlas & Gazetteer*: Page 53 A8

The Hike

You'll love hiking through this 898-acre park filled with orchards, large open fields, and pockets of forest, sloughs, and waterways. Originally this park was made up of two islands in the Willamette River. In 1861 a catastrophic flood occurred; when the floodwaters receded, an abundance of topsoil was left behind, causing the two islands to join. The original homesteader on Brown Island was Isaac Whiskey Brown, who grew tobacco and raised livestock. John Minto, an early homesteader and legislator, purchased 247 acres and settled on neighboring Minto Island in 1867.

Currently the park is managed by the Salem Regional Park and Recreation Agency as a wildlife and recreation area that features more than 20 miles of paved and unpaved pathways. It is an important wintering area for dusky Canada geese, which arrive at the refuge in mid-October and stay through mid-April. Look for the geese in the park's open fields and waterways. Commercial agriculture crops are still grown on the island. More than 244 acres are planted each year in such crops as potatoes, sweet corn, snap beans, and wheat.

This easy 5.8-mile loop is a combination of paved and dirt paths that take you next to the Willamette River; through shady wooded areas past sloughs and ponds; and through large, sunny pastures and fields. Your canine partner will be glad to know that the park also has a twenty-acre leash-free area, located in a large grassy field surrounded by bunches of deciduous trees. Rover will never grow tired of playing Frisbee or fetch in this huge outdoor playground. To reach the leash-free area, turn right onto Minto Island Road and travel 0.5 mile to a gravel parking area on the left side of the road.

The hike described here is only one of dozens of possible routes you can explore. You can try this route or create your own.

Miles and Directions

0.0   Start hiking on the paved trail that starts to the left of the restrooms at the far end of the parking area.

0.1   Walk over a wooden bridge and arrive at an intersection with a paved road. Turn right and continue on the paved route marked by a BIKE ROUTE sign.

0.3   Turn left at the trail junction and continue on the paved trail.

0.6   Turn right at the trail junction and continue hiking on the flat, paved path. Enter a shady corridor of stately cottonwood trees.

1.3   Veer right at the trail junction (a dirt path heads left at this junction), and continue on the paved path that passes through a large grove of cottonwoods.

1.5   The paved path begins paralleling the Willamette River. (FYI: Watch for dusky Canada geese, blue herons, and other birds along this section of the route.)

2.1   Turn left (away from the river) and continue walking on the paved trail. (FYI: A dirt trail heads right).

2.2   Arrive at a T-intersection with a paved trail. Veer right and continue on the paved path. (After this turn there is a parking area on the left and restrooms on the right side of the trail.)

2.3   Arrive at a trail junction. Go right on the paved path as it skirts the right side of the picnic area.

2.4   Turn right onto a paved path.

2.5   Turn right at the trail junction and continue on the paved path. (FYI: The trail parallels a slough on the right.)

2.7   Turn left at the trail junction and continue hiking on the paved path.

2.9   Turn right and continue on the paved path.

3.0   Veer right and continue on the paved path.

3.3   Continue straight (left). (A side trail heading right crosses a bridge.)

3.5 Turn left onto a dirt path. (The paved trail heads right at this junction).

4.1 Walk past the Salem Golf Club on your right.

4.3 Turn right onto a paved path.

4.7 Turn right onto a paved path.

4.8 Turn right onto a paved path.

5.3 Pass a large pond on your right.

5.7 The paved path intersects Minto Island Road. Cross the road and then turn right onto the paved path on the other side.

5.8 Turn left into the parking area and return to the trailhead.

14 Willamette Mission State Park

This easy, serene route takes you on a tour past the scenic Willamette River, Mission Lake, and what is thought to be the world's biggest black cottonwood tree. You can follow the route described here or design your own route on the park's many trails.

Distance: 2.3-mile loop (with other options)

Approximate hiking time: 1 hour

Elevation gain: None

Trail surface: Dirt path, paved path

Best season: Year-round

Other trail users: Joggers, cyclists, equestrians

Canine compatibility: Leashed dogs permitted

Fees and permits: Day-use fee

Schedule: Open dawn to dusk

Maps: USGS: Mission Bottom; Maptech CD: Newport/Portland/ Mount Hood/The Dalles; Willamette Mission State Park trail map available from Oregon State Parks (800-551-6969; www .oregonstateparks.org/park_139 .php)

Trail contact: Oregon State Parks and Recreation, 725 Summer Street NE, Suite C, Salem 97301; (800) 551-6949; www.oregon .gov/ORPD/PARKS/index.shtml

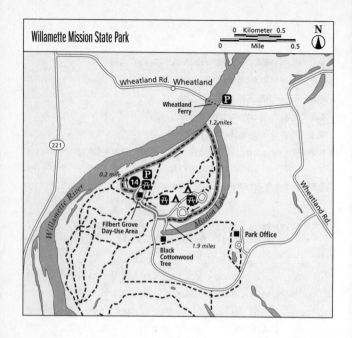

Willamette Mission State Park

0 Kilometer 0.5

0 Mile 0.5

N

Wheatland Rd. Wheatland

Wheatland Ferry

P

1.2 miles

221

0.2 mile

14 P

Willamette River

Filbert Grove Day-Use Area

Mission Lake

Park Office

1.9 miles

Black Cottonwood Tree

Wheatland Rd.

Finding the trailhead: From Interstate 5 take exit 263 toward Brooks and Gervais. (This exit is approximately 8 miles south of Woodburn and 9 miles north of Salem.) At the end of the off-ramp, set your mileage indicator to "0." Turn west onto Brooklake Road and go 1.6 miles to the intersection with Wheatland Road. Turn right onto Wheatland Road and drive 2.4 miles to the entrance road to Willamette Mission State Park. Turn left onto the park entrance road and drive 0.6 mile to the pay booth for the park. (You'll need to pay a day-use fee. If an attendant is not in the pay booth, you can purchase a permit from the self-pay machine located at the entrance booth.) Continue 1.2 miles (staying to the left at each road junction) to the Filbert Grove Day-Use Area. *DeLorme: Oregon Atlas & Gazetteer:* Page 59 D8

The Hike

This hike begins in historic Willamette Mission State Park, which has expansive lawns and picnic areas, multiuse trails, walnut and filbert orchards, and picturesque meadowlands. This state park is the location of the Willamette Station of the Methodist Mission that was established by Reverend Jason Lee in 1834. After his arrival, Lee and other missionaries built a one-room school, chapel, kitchen, and living quarters. In addition, thirty acres of ground were prepared for planting. After only two years, the mission was teaching Indian children and was becoming self-sufficient. By 1837 the first white women arrived in the Willamette Valley. One of these women, Anna Maria Pittman, married Jason Lee. In 1840 the main mission was moved from the floodplain to Salem. In 1861 the Willamette River flooded and destroyed most of the original mission. Today none of the original buildings stand, but the Jason Lee Willamette Mission Monument, located adjacent to Mission Lake, marks the site of the original settlement. Beautiful pink roses growing next to the monument are from some of the mission's original plants.

This hike begins by following a paved bike path that parallels the Willamette River. Watch for blue herons and Canada geese feeding along the water's edge. After 1.2 miles you'll follow a wide doubletrack road along the shores of Mission Lake. The smooth waters of this lake are popular with kayakers. After 1.9 miles you'll get to glimpse a very large black cottonwood tree. This stately tree is more than 250 years old, is more than 156 feet tall, and measures 26 feet 8 inches in circumference. You'll finish the hike by walking on a quiet paved road for 0.4 mile back to your starting point.

Miles and Directions

0.0 Start hiking on the trail adjacent to the restrooms located at the far northwest corner of the parking area.

0.2 Turn right onto the paved bike path that parallels the wide, lazy Willamette River.

1.2 Turn right onto a grassy doubletrack road. Soon you'll pass Mission Lake on your left. Continue through a walnut orchard, staying to the left at all trail junctions.

1.9 Arrive at a paved road and a sign that points to the world's largest black cottonwood tree. Continue on the paved road for 0.4 mile; at the first road junction go left, and at the second road junction go right.

2.3 Arrive back at your starting point.

15 Silver Falls State Park

This gorgeous singletrack path weaves through Silver Creek Canyon past many spectacular waterfalls in Silver Falls State Park. The trail starts next to South Falls Lodge and descends steeply into the canyon. Immediately you'll have a grand view of 177-foot South Falls—one of the park's best-known waterfalls. Before you know it, the trail takes you behind the falls into a unique basalt cave. The cooling spray from the sweeping cascade is a welcome relief on a hot summer's day. The trail continues to travel along the South Fork of Silver Creek through a forest of bigleaf maple, sword fern, and Douglas fir. After passing several more waterfalls, the trail follows the North Fork of Silver Creek, continuing past more gorgeous canyon scenery. You'll finish the loop high on the rim on the Rim Trail, which takes you through more shady pine forest.

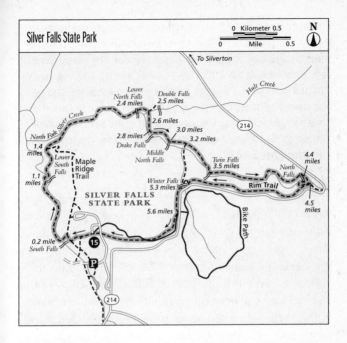

Silver Falls State Park

0 Kilometer 0.5
0 Mile 0.5
N

To Silverton

Hult Creek

Lower North Falls 2.4 miles
Double Falls 2.5 miles

2.6 miles

North Fork Silver Creek

1.4 miles

2.8 miles
Drake Falls

3.0 miles
3.2 miles

Lower South Falls

Maple Ridge Trail

Middle North Falls

Twin Falls 3.5 miles

North Falls

4.4 miles

1.1 miles

SILVER FALLS STATE PARK

Winter Falls 5.3 miles

Rim Trail

4.5 miles

5.6 miles

Bike Path

0.2 mile South Falls

15

P

214

Distance: 6.9-mile loop
Approximate hiking time: 2.5 to 3.5 hours
Elevation gain: 515 feet
Trail surface: Dirt path, paved path
Best season: Year-round
Other trail users: None
Canine compatibility: Dogs not permitted on this specific hike, which includes the Canyon, Maple Ridge, and Winter Trails; leashed dogs permitted on other trails in the park

Fees and permits: Day-use fee
Schedule: Open dawn to dusk
Maps: USGS: Drake Crossing; Maptech CD: Newport/Portland/Mount Hood/The Dalles; Silver Falls State Park trail map available from Oregon State Parks (800-551-6949; www.oregon stateparks.org/images/pdf/silverfalls_trailmap.pdf)
Trail contact: Oregon State Parks and Recreation, 725 Summer Street NE, Suite C, Salem 97301; (800) 551-6949; www.oregon .gov/ORPD/PARKS/index.shtml

Finding the trailhead: From Interstate 5 in Salem, turn east onto Highway 22 toward North Santiam Highway-Stayton-Detroit Lake. Travel 5 miles east and take exit 7 onto Highway 214 toward Silver Falls State Park. At the end of the off-ramp, turn left onto Highway 214 and continue 4.5 miles to a stop sign. Turn left at the stop sign and travel 12.2 miles on Highway 214 to the entrance to Silver Falls State Park. After entering the park, turn left at the South Falls turnoff. Proceed to the parking area and trailhead. *DeLorme: Oregon Atlas & Gazetteer:* Page 54 A3

The Hike

Silver Falls State Park—at 9,000 acres, Oregon's largest state park—is a canyon carved by the North and South Forks of Silver Creek and is loaded with waterfalls. It's thought that the creeks are named for James "Silver" Smith, who traveled to the area with his pockets full of silver coins in the 1840s. The name lived on when Silver Falls was established in the 1880s—then consisting of nothing more than a sawmill, a hotel, and several hunting lodges. The land was overzealously logged for its timber until the late 1920s, when the state considered turning the area into a national park. The logging ground to a halt, but unfortunately national park status was never realized. The land had been subjected to too much logging and farming and didn't pass muster for the National Park Service. The federal government purchased the land during the Depression and designated it as a Recreational Demonstration Area featuring recreational facilities, hiking trails, and the South Falls Lodge. All of what you'll find here was built by the Civilian Conservation Corps.

This 6.9-mile loop takes you beneath a forested canyon of stately Douglas fir, western hemlock, red cedar, maple, alder, and cottonwoods and many cascading waterfalls. In fall the maples are colored in brilliant reds, oranges, and yellows that contrast sharply with the dark green of the surrounding forest.

Miles and Directions

0.0 From the parking area begin hiking on a paved cobble path toward South Falls Lodge.

0.1 Turn left onto the Canyon Trail as it descends steeply into the Silver Creek Canyon. (FYI: As you descend you'll have a gorgeous view of 177-foot South Falls.)

0.2 Turn left and go behind the falls into a cool basalt cave.

0.3 Veer left and continue on the well-traveled path. The path turns to dirt at this junction.

1.1 Admire 93-foot Lower South Falls.

1.4 Continue straight (left). (The Maple Ridge Trail heads right.)

2.4 Arrive at 30-foot Lower North Falls. Go several yards farther and head left to view 178-foot Double Falls.

2.5 Arrive at Double Falls. After viewing the falls, turn around and head back to the main trail.

2.6 Turn left onto the main trail and cross a footbridge over Hult Creek.

2.8 Pass the short, fat cascade of Drake Falls.

3.0 Enjoy views of 103-foot Middle North Falls.

3.2 Continue straight (left). (The trail that heads right goes to Winter Falls.)

3.5 Pass 31-foot Twin Falls.

4.4 Arrive at your last waterfall on the route, 136-foot North Falls. Walk behind the falls and then ascend a steep set of concrete stairs leading to the canyon rim.

4.5 Turn sharply to the right and continue on the Rim Trail. (**Option:** Continue straight (left) and continue 0.2 mile to view Upper North Falls.)

5.3 Continue straight where a sign states SOUTH FALLS TRAILHEAD 1.6 MILES. Walk through a paved parking area and then continue following the trail.

5.6 Turn right at the trail fork.

6.1 Turn right at the trail fork.

6.8 Cross a paved road.

6.9 Arrive back at the trailhead parking area at South Falls.

16 Clackamas River Trail

This beautiful river trail takes you on a mystical journey through pockets of mossy old-growth forest that will astound you. This trail hides immense Douglas fir and western red cedar giants and offers grand views of the Clackamas River at several viewpoints. Additional highlights include a viewpoint of Pup Creek Falls and opportunities to go for a swim.

Distance: 8.0 miles one-way (with a shuttle)
Approximate hiking time: 3 to 4 hours one way; 6 to 8 hours out and back
Elevation gain: 520 feet
Trail surface: Dirt path
Best season: Open year-round; driest months, June through October
Other trail users: None
Canine compatibility: Leashed dogs permitted
Fees and permits: Northwest Forest Pass required; passes available by calling (800) 270-7504 or online at www.fs.fed.us/r6/passespermits
Schedule: Open all hours
Maps: USGS: Fish Creek Mountain, Three Lynx, Bedford Point; Maptech CD: Newport/Portland/Mount Hood/The Dalles
Trail contact: Mount Hood National Forest, Estacada Ranger Station, 595 Northwest Industrial Way, Estacada 97023; (503) 630-6861; www.fs.fed.us/r6/mthood

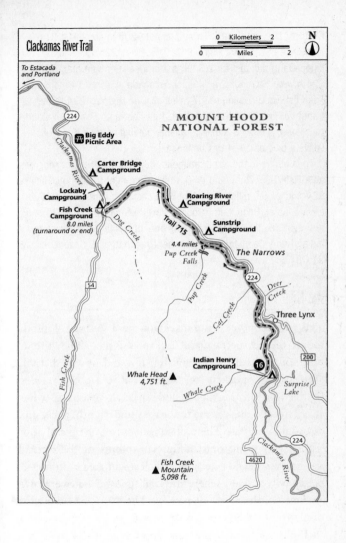

Clackamas River Trail

0   Kilometers   2

0   Miles   2

N

MOUNT HOOD NATIONAL FOREST

To Estacada and Portland

224

Big Eddy Picnic Area

Carter Bridge Campground

Lockaby Campground

Fish Creek Campground
8.0 miles
(turnaround or end)

Clackamas River

Dog Creek

Roaring River Campground

Trail 715

Sunstrip Campground

4.4 miles
Pup Creek Falls

The Narrows

224

Deer Creek

54

Pup Creek

Cat Creek

Three Lynx

Fish Creek

200

Indian Henry Campground

16

Whale Head
4,751 ft.

Whale Creek

Surprise Lake

224

Fish Creek Mountain
5,098 ft.

4620

Clackamas River

Finding the trailhead: From Interstate 205 in southeast Portland, take exit 12A for Highway 212/Highway 224/Clackamas/Estacada. Head east for 3.5 miles and then veer right onto Highway 224 toward Estacada. You'll reach Estacada in about 14 more miles. From Estacada continue 14.7 miles east on Highway 224 to the turnoff for Fish Creek Campground. Turn right onto Fish Creek Road (unsigned) and go 0.3 mile to a large parking area on the right. Leave a bike or car at this trailhead.

To continue to the upper trailhead, turn left out of the parking area onto Fish Creek Road and go 0.3 mile. Turn right (east) onto Highway 224 and go 6.6 miles. Turn right onto unsigned Forest Road 4620 toward Indian Henry Campground. Travel 0.6 mile on FR 4620 and turn right into the trailhead parking area opposite the entrance to Indian Henry Campground. *DeLorme: Oregon Atlas & Gazetteer:* Page 61 D8

The Hike

This fantastic river route takes you on a journey along the shores of the spectacular Clackamas River. The first 2.9 miles of the trail have many fun ups and downs that take you through pockets of magnificent old-growth forest. Distractions on the trail include a basalt overhang, where you'll have to duck as the trail passes underneath, and a small cascading waterfall. The trail continues rolling up and down ridges with many outstanding viewpoints of the river. It also weaves in and out of an old clear-cut area with not-so-pretty power lines, where the trail tends to be overgrown. As you continue, you'll pass by The Narrows—a narrow basalt gorge where the river rushes through a 20-foot-wide rock channel. After you cross Pup Creek at 4.4 miles, you have the option of turning left and walking 200 yards to a viewpoint of Pup Creek Falls. At 7.3 miles look for a sandy beach where you can take a swim on a hot summer day. After 8.0 miles you'll cross Fish Creek Road and arrive at a trailhead parking area and your shuttle vehicle (or turn-around point if you've done this as an out-and-back hike).

Miles and Directions

0.0 Begin hiking on the singletrack trail at a wood trail sign. Almost immediately, you'll need to turn right as the trail passes through a cool, mossy forest.

4.4 Cross Pup Creek over a rock path. (**Side trip:** Just after crossing the creek, turn left and head 200 yards up a side trail to view the feathery cascade of Pup Creek Falls.)

7.3 Pass a tantalizing sandy beach that may tempt you to stop and take a swim on a hot day.

8.0 The trail intersects Fish Creek Road and the end of the route. Cross Fish Creek Road to the trailhead parking area and your shuttle vehicle.

17 Riverside Trail

This beautiful off-the-beaten-path river trail offers stunning views of the Clackamas River and opportunities to view immense red cedars and features superb swimming holes.

Distance: 8.4 miles out and back

Approximate hiking time: 3 to 4 hours

Elevation gain: 170 feet

Trail surface: Dirt path, wood bridges

Best season: Open year-round; driest months, June through October

Other trail users: Mountain bikers

Canine compatibility: Leashed dogs permitted

Fees and permits: Northwest Forest Pass required; passes available by calling (800) 270-7504 or online at www.fs.fed.us/r6/passespermits

Schedule: Open all hours

Maps: USGS: Fish Creek Mountain; Maptech CD: Newport/Portland/Mount Hood/The Dalles

Trail contact: Mount Hood National Forest, Estacada Ranger Station, 595 Northwest Industrial Way, Estacada 97023; (503) 630-6861; www.fs.fed.us/r6/mthood

Finding the trailhead: From Interstate 205 in southeast Portland, take exit 12A for Highway 212/Highway 224/Clackamas/Estacada. Head east for 3.5 miles and then veer right onto Highway 224 toward Estacada. You'll reach Estacada in about 14 more miles. From Estacada, continue 25 miles east on Highway 224 to a road junction (right after you cross the Oak Grove Fork of the Clackamas River). Continue right toward Detroit/Bagby Hot Springs on Forest Road 46. Almost immediately after making this turn, veer right into Rainbow Campground. Continue 0.3 mile through the campground to the trailhead at the end of the campground loop road. *DeLorme: Oregon Atlas & Gazetteer:* Page 66 D8

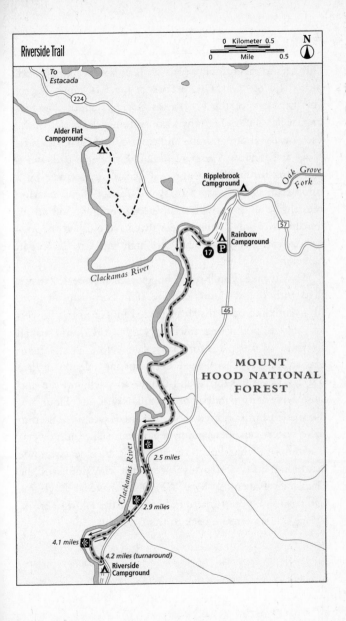

Riverside Trail

0 Kilometer 0.5
0 Mile 0.5

N

To Estacada

(224)

Alder Flat Campground

Ripplebrook Campground

Oak Grove Fork

57

Rainbow Campground

17

P

Clackamas River

46

MOUNT HOOD NATIONAL FOREST

Clackamas River

2.5 miles

2.9 miles

4.1 miles

4.2 miles (turnaround)

Riverside Campground

The Hike

This scenic river trail begins at Rainbow Campground, located on the Oak Grove Fork of the Clackamas River. This tributary of the Clackamas River is about 25 miles long; it flows into Timothy Lake and then flows out of the reservoir for about 16 miles and empties into the Clackamas River at Rainbow Campground. The riverside path twists and turns through immense red cedars surrounded by a shimmering green carpet of sword ferns. These amazing trees thrive in areas with a moist environment and are in demand by lumber mills. Trees that have escaped the logger's ax can grow to be 200 feet high and 8 to 10 feet in diameter.

As you hike, you'll pass a boggy area at Mile 1.4 that is filled with yellow skunk cabbage. This curious plant gives off a skunklike odor that is produced by sap in the flowers and attracts pollinating insects. Native Americans soaked the roots of this plant for many days before eating them. This soaking process helped leech out the calcium oxalate that can cause the throat and tongue to swell and can also cause temporary paralysis of the salivary glands. Flour was also made from the dried roots, and the leaves were used to make water containers and to relieve headaches and fevers.

Additional highlights on this trail include awesome swimming holes and many spectacular viewpoints of the Clackamas River. At Mile 4.2 you'll arrive at Riverside Campground (your turnaround point). After taking a break, retrace the same route back to the trailhead.

Miles and Directions

0.0 Start by hiking south on the singletrack trail. Cross a creek with some large boulders.

2.5 Pass a great viewpoint of the Clackamas River.

2.6 Cross a wood bridge over a side creek. After crossing the bridge, turn right and continue on the track signed RIVERSIDE TRAIL #723.

2.9 Pass another great viewpoint of the Clackamas River.

3.1 Continue straight (left).

3.6 Pass an inviting swimming beach.

4.0 Pass another great swimming hole.

4.1 Arrive at the crest of a hill giving you a commanding view of the river. From here begin a steep descent.

4.2 Reach Riverside Campground (your turnaround point). (FYI: Restrooms and water are available here.) Retrace the same route back to your starting point.

8.4 Arrive back at the trailhead.

18 Larch Mountain Crater–Sherrard Point

This short trail takes you to the rocky promontory of Sherrard Point on the summit of Larch Mountain. From this summit vantage point you'll have outstanding views of the Columbia River Gorge, Mount Rainier, Mount Adams, Mount St. Helens, Mount Hood, and Mount Jefferson.

Distance: 0.5 mile out and back
Approximate hiking time: 15 to 30 minutes
Elevation gain: 130 feet
Trail surface: Paved path
Best season: Year-round
Other trail users: None
Canine compatibility: Leashed dogs permitted
Fees and permits: No fees or permits required

Schedule: Open all hours
Maps: USGS: Multnomah Falls; Maptech CD: Newport/Portland/Mount Hood/The Dalles
Trail contact: USDA Forest Service, Columbia River Gorge National Scenic Area, 902 Wasco Avenue, Suite 200, Hood River 97031; (541) 308-1700; www.fs.fed.us/r6/columbia

Finding the trailhead: From the intersection of Interstates 205 and 84 in Portland, drive 9 miles east on I-84 to exit 18 for Lewis & Clark State Park. At the end of the off-ramp, turn left onto the Columbia River Highway. Continue 0.5 mile and arrive at a stop sign and intersection. Turn left where a sign indicates Historic Highway, Corbett, Dabney State Park. Proceed 4 miles on the Historic Columbia River Highway to a road fork. Go right where a sign indicates HISTORIC HIGHWAY/CORBETT/MULTNOMAH FALLS, and travel 4.5 miles to another road fork. Continue straight (right) on Larch Mountain Road and go 15.5 miles to the Larch Mountain Picnic Area and parking lot. *DeLorme: Oregon Atlas & Gazetteer:* Page 67 D8

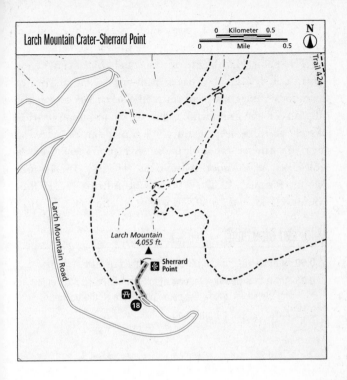

The Hike

As the westernmost high point in the Columbia River Gorge, 4,055-foot Larch Mountain is a spectacular natural area and offers some of the best views of the Columbia River Gorge and the surrounding Cascade Mountain peaks from its lofty summit. Douglas, silver, and noble firs grace its slopes along with a thick understory of sword, licorice, and maidenhair ferns. Ironically, no larch trees grow on Larch Mountain—these trees typically grow only on the eastern side of the Cascades. Loggers often mistakenly called the noble fir a "larch," which led to the misleading name.

This short hike begins at the Larch Mountain Picnic Area. You'll walk on a paved path and ascend a series of stairs to a viewpoint platform atop Sherrard Point on the summit of the mountain. This rocky promontory rises sharply above a deep, extinct volcano. From the viewing area you can see (on a clear day) five prominent Cascade volcanoes: 8,363-foot Mount St. Helens, 14,410-foot Mount Rainier, 12,276-foot Mount Adams, 11,235-foot Mount Hood, and 10,497-foot Mount Jefferson.

Miles and Directions

0.00 Start walking on the paved trail, signed SHERRARD POINT.

0.25 Arrive at a viewing platform atop Sherrard Point. After enjoying the views, follow the same path back to the trailhead.

0.50 Arrive back at the trailhead.

19 Latourell Falls

This loop route takes you on a tour of Upper and Lower Latourell Falls in the Columbia River Gorge National Scenic Area. The route travels through a scenic creek canyon filled with colorful wildflowers and wild berries. Additional highlights include opportunities to wade in the creek and have a picnic at a shady picnic area near the trail's end.

Distance: 2.3-mile loop
Approximate hiking time: 1 hour
Elevation gain: 425 feet
Trail surface: Paved path, dirt path
Best season: Year-round
Other trail users: None
Canine compatibility: Leashed dogs permitted
Fees and permits: No fees or permits required

Schedule: Open all hours
Maps: USGS: Bridal Veil; Maptech CD: Newport/Portland/Mount Hood/The Dalles
Trail contact: USDA Forest Service, Columbia River Gorge National Scenic Area, 902 Wasco Avenue, Suite 200, Hood River 97031; (541) 308-1700; www.fs.fed.us/r6/columbia

Finding the trailhead: From the intersection of Interstates 205 and 84 in Portland, travel about 18.5 miles east on I-84 to exit 28 for Bridal Veil Falls. Continue 0.4 mile to a stop sign at the intersection with the Historic Columbia River Highway. Turn right (west) onto the Historic Columbia River Highway and travel 2.7 miles to the Latourell Falls parking area, located on the left side of the highway. *DeLorme: Oregon Atlas & Gazetteer:* Page 67 D7

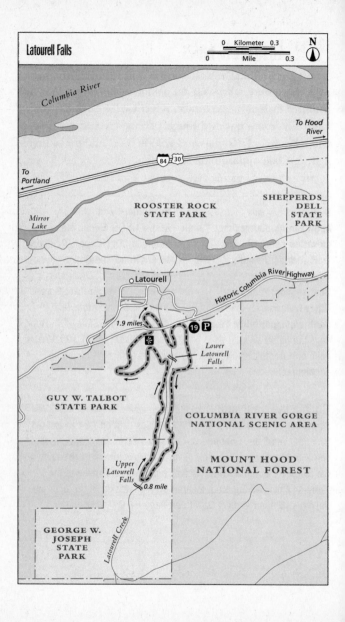

The Hike

This loop trail takes you on a gorgeous waterfall tour of Upper and Lower Latourell Falls in Guy W. Talbot State Park, located in the Columbia River Gorge. Catastrophic floods sculpted this magnificent river gorge near the end of the last ice age (12,000 to 19,000 years ago). These floods were created when the climate began to warm up, causing 2,000-foot ice dams that held 3,000-square-mile Lake Missoula in Montana to break. The floods poured through eastern Washington and then in a southwest direction across the Columbia Plateau and finally escaped through the Columbia River drainage, widening the valley floor and carving the cliffs you see today. As a result of these floods, the lower courses of many of the valley's tributary streams were cut off, creating an area with spectacular waterfalls.

The trail heads left from the parking area and takes you 0.3 mile to a viewpoint of the shimmering cascade of 249-foot Lower Latourell Falls. From the viewpoint continue about 0.5 mile through thick undergrowth of vine maple, wild raspberry, and sword fern to the 100-foot cascade of Upper Latourell Falls. From the upper falls, the trail descends 0.5 mile to a scenic viewpoint of the Columbia River Gorge. Keep following the trail as it continues downhill to the highway. Cross the highway and follow a path through a picturesque picnic area. Bear right at the trail junction and follow the paved path as it heads under the Historic Columbia River Highway and leads you along the edge of the creek to a viewpoint of the feathery cascade of Lower Latourell Falls. Continue back to your starting point at 2.3 miles.

Note: This hike can be crowded on summer weekends.

Miles and Directions

0.0 Start hiking on the paved trail that heads uphill from the parking area. Ascend 100 yards and arrive at a scenic viewpoint of Lower Latourell Falls. Continue on the trail as it switchbacks steeply uphill.

0.8 Cross a footbridge over a creek. Admire the swirling cascade of Upper Latourell Falls as it plunges into a deep rock pool. Continue on the trail as it descends, paralleling the creek.

1.9 Cross the Historic Columbia River Highway and continue on the paved trail on the other side. At a four-way junction, continue straight (left) and head downhill. You'll pass through a shady picnic area. At the next trail fork (before a paved road), turn right and continue walking on the paved trail as it goes underneath the highway. Soon you'll arrive at a footbridge that crosses the creek near the base of Lower Latourell Falls. Enjoy the view of the falls and continue on the paved trail back to your starting point.

2.3 Arrive back at the trailhead and parking area.

20 Bridal Veil Falls

This 0.9-mile easy ramble takes you on a tour of two trails in Bridal Veil Falls State Park in the Columbia River Gorge. You'll begin on the Overlook Loop Trail, which offers commanding views of the Columbia River Gorge and meanders through a wildflower meadow filled with the rare camas plant. The route continues on the Bridal Veil Falls Trail, which descends into a shady creek canyon and takes you to a grand viewpoint of Bridal Veil Falls.

Distance: 0.9 mile out and back

Approximate hiking time: 30 to 45 minutes

Elevation gain: 100 feet

Trail surface: Paved path and dirt path

Best season: Year-round

Other trail users: None

Canine compatibility: Leashed dogs permitted

Fees and permits: No fees or permits required

Schedule: Open all hours.

Maps: USGS: Bridal Veil; Maptech CD: Newport/Portland/Mount Hood/The Dalles

Trail contact: USDA Forest Service, Columbia River Gorge National Scenic Area, 902 Wasco Avenue, Suite 200, Hood River 97031; (541) 308-1700; www.fs.fed.us/r6/columbia

Finding the trailhead: From the intersection of Interstates 205 and 84 in Portland, travel about 18.5 miles east on I-84 to exit 28 (Bridal Veil Falls). Continue 0.4 mile to a stop sign at the intersection with the Historic Columbia River Highway. Turn right (west) onto the Historic Columbia River Highway and travel 0.8 mile to Bridal Veil State Park, located on the right side of the highway. *DeLorme: Oregon Atlas & Gazetteer:* Page 67 D7

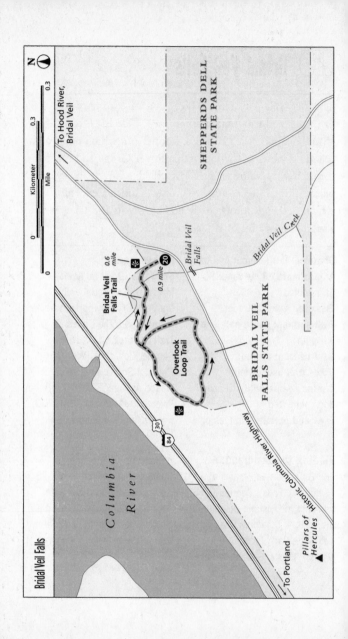

Bridal Veil Falls

The Hike

This state park features a picturesque picnic area and two scenic hiking trails. You'll begin the hike on the Overlook Loop Trail, which passes through a thick undergrowth of wild raspberries, bright purple lupine, other wildflowers, ferns, and vine maple. After 0.1 mile you'll pass an interpretive sign on the left that describes the Native Peoples that have lived here for more than 10,000 years. The Columbia River allowed the Chinookan-speaking people to travel via canoe and was an important trade route between the coast and the central and eastern parts of the state. Traders gathered here from all over the Northwest at large fairlike events that featured gambling, games, races, dances, and ceremonial displays.

The Native Peoples' primary food source was salmon, supplemented with native plants including wapato, camas, nuts, a variety of berries, and wild game. As you continue on this trail, you'll pass through one of the largest remaining meadows of camas in the western part of the Columbia River Gorge. This plant, 6 to 24 inches tall, can be identified by its beautiful blue flowers that bloom from mid-April to May. Camas has a small bulb that Native Americans baked in earth ovens and then pressed into cakes. Pioneers also dined on the camas plant and took care not to confuse it with the white-flowered toxic death camas. Other wildflowers you'll see on this trail include Oregon iris, checker lily, the bright orange globes of the tiger lily, and cliff penstemon.

As you continue on the trail, you'll pass more viewpoints of the Columbia River Gorge. The Overlook Loop Trail ends at the parking lot after 0.3 mile. The route continues on the Bridal Veil Falls Trail, which travels through thick stands of bigleaf maple, sword fern, vine maple, yarrow, wild roses, bright purple lupine, and wild raspberries. At 0.4 mile the paved trail becomes gravel and begins descending into a creek canyon. After 0.6 mile you'll cross a bridge over a bubbling creek. Continue up a series of stairs to a viewpoint of the billowy cascade of Bridal Veil Falls before retracing your route.

Note: This popular hike can be crowded on summer weekends.

Miles and Directions

0.0 From the parking area look for a sign that notes TRAIL TO FALLS. Walk on a paved path next to the sign for about 20 feet to a trail junction. Turn left and continue on a paved path where a sign indicates OVERLOOK LOOP TRAIL. (FYI: Restrooms and water are on the left side of the trail about 30 feet from this junction.)

0.1 Pass an interpretive sign on the right that describes the history of the Native Peoples of the Columbia River Gorge.

0.2 Turn right onto a side path that leads to a scenic viewpoint of the gorge. Head back to the main trail and turn right. At the next trail junction, turn right to another scenic viewpoint and interpretive sign that describes the development of the Historic Columbia River Highway. Return to the main trail and turn right. Continue through a picnic area shaded by large oak trees to the main parking area and your starting point.

0.3 Arrive at the parking area. Continue the hike by picking up the paved path at the far end of the parking area. At the first trail junction, turn right at the Bridal Veil Falls Trail sign.

0.6 Cross a wood footbridge over a creek and walk up a series of stairs to a wood platform to view the shimmering cascade of Bridal Veil Falls. Retrace the same route back to the trailhead.

0.9 Arrive back at the trailhead.

21 Elowah Falls–Upper McCord Creek Falls

This hike takes you on a tour of stunning Elowah Falls and McCord Creek Falls in John B. Yeon State Park in the Columbia River Gorge.

Distance: 3.2 miles round-trip
Approximate hiking time: 1 to 1.5 hours
Elevation gain: 485 feet
Trail surface: Dirt path
Best season: Year-round
Other trail users: None
Canine compatibility: Leashed dogs permitted
Fees and permits: No fees or permits required

Schedule: Open all hours
Maps: USGS: Tanner Butte; Maptech CD: Newport/Portland/Mount Hood/The Dalles
Trail contact: Oregon State Parks and Recreation, 725 Summer Street NE, Suite C, Salem 97301; (800) 551-6949; www .oregon.gov/ORPD/PARKS/index .shtml

Finding the trailhead: From the junction of Interstates 205 and Interstate 84 in Portland, travel east on I-84 for 27.3 miles to exit 35 for Ainsworth State Park. At the stop sign go left (west) on the Historic Columbia River Highway toward Dodson/Warrendale/Hood River. Go 2.2 miles to the John B. Yeon State Park parking area, located on the right side of the road. *DeLorme: Oregon Atlas & Gazetteer:* Page 68 C1

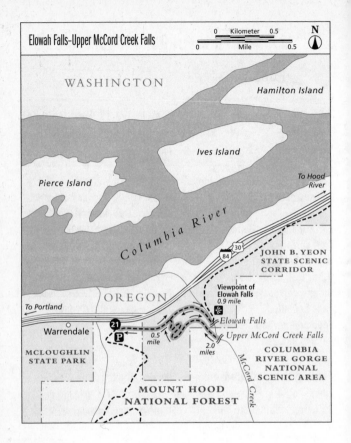

Elowah Falls–Upper McCord Creek Falls

0   Kilometer   0.5

0   Mile   0.5

N

WASHINGTON

Hamilton Island

Ives Island

Pierce Island

Columbia River

To Hood River

30 84

JOHN B. YEON STATE SCENIC CORRIDOR

OREGON

Viewpoint of Elowah Falls
0.9 mile

Elowah Falls

Upper McCord Creek Falls

To Portland

Warrendale

21 P *0.5 mile*

2.0 miles

McCord Creek

COLUMBIA RIVER GORGE NATIONAL SCENIC AREA

MCLOUGHLIN STATE PARK

MOUNT HOOD NATIONAL FOREST

The Hike

The 3.2-mile round-trip hike to Elowah Falls and Upper McCord Creek Falls is a great introduction to some of the beautiful waterfalls in the Columbia River Gorge. From the parking area walk 0.1 mile up the trail and turn left toward Elowah Falls. After 0.4 mile of walking beneath a shady forested canopy, you'll arrive at a trail junction. Turn left and continue 0.4 mile to a viewpoint of the impressive cascade of Elowah Falls. From here retrace the same route 0.4 mile back to a trail junction, and turn left toward Upper McCord Creek Falls. Follow the trail as it switchbacks steeply up a fern-covered hillside and follow it for 0.7 mile to a viewpoint of Upper McCord Creek Falls. There is a small section with a handrail just before you reach the falls. Enjoy the view of the falls as it splashes down a steep creek canyon, and then head back on the same trail to the parking area.

Miles and Directions

0.0 Start hiking from the parking area on the marked trail.

0.1 Turn left toward Elowah Falls.

0.5 Turn left at the trail junction.

0.9 Arrive at Elowah Falls. After enjoying the view, turn around and head back to the last trail junction.

1.3 Turn left toward Upper McCord Creek Falls.

1.9 Use caution as you approach the falls. The trail becomes narrow; use the handrail if you feel unsteady.

2.0 Arrive at a viewpoint of Upper McCord Creek Falls. After enjoying the view, turn around and head back on the same route to a trail junction.

2.7 Turn left at the trail junction.

3.1 Turn right at the trail junction.

3.2 Arrive back at the trailhead.

22 Wahclella Falls

This short hike takes you along the edge of Tanner Creek to a roaring two-tiered waterfall that plunges into a deep rocky pool. Shady maples, wild raspberries, and splashes of wildflowers decorate this fun, family hike. An optional loop takes you down to the creek's edge, where you can wade in the cool, clear water on hot summer days.

Distance: 2.2 miles out and back (with optional loop)
Approximate hiking time: 1 hour
Elevation gain: 300 feet
Trail surface: Gravel path, stairs
Best season: Year-round
Other trail users: None
Canine compatibility: Leashed dogs permitted
Fees and permits: Northwest Forest Pass required; passes available by calling (800) 270-

7504 or online at www.fs.fed.us/r6/passespermits
Schedule: Open all hours
Maps: USGS: Bonneville Dam; Maptech CD: Newport/Portland/Mount Hood/The Dalles
Trail contact: USDA Forest Service, Columbia River Gorge National Scenic Area, 902 Wasco Avenue, Suite 200, Hood River 97031; (541) 308-1700; www.fs.fed.us/r6/columbia

Finding the trailhead: From Portland head east on Interstate 84 for about 40 miles to exit 40 for Bonneville Dam. At the stop sign, turn right and pull into the gravel parking lot at the Wahclella Falls trailhead. *DeLorme: Oregon Atlas & Gazetteer:* Page 68 C1

The Hike

The Columbia River Gorge has many scenic hiking trails that wind through mossy, green forests and lead you to spectacular ridgetops and cascading waterfalls. The gorge has

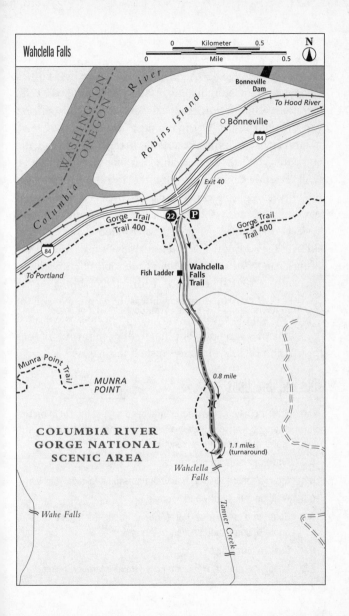

one of the highest concentrations of waterfalls in the United States. More than seventy-seven falls make a roaring dive over basalt cliffs in a 420-square-mile area. The best-known waterfall in the Columbia River Gorge is Multnomah Falls. The long, thin, two-tiered cascade of this magnificent waterfall plunges 620 feet into a deep, rocky pool.

This concentration of amazing waterfalls is due to the 2,000- to 3,000-foot basalt cliffs that line the gorge. Huge basalt lava flows poured through the area ten to seventeen million years ago, creeping toward the sea. For millions of years the Columbia River has been carving the beautiful gorge you see today. A few massive floods (we're talking geologic proportions) following periods of glaciation made abrupt changes in the landscape. One such flood occurred as recently as 13,000 years ago. A natural dam broke on the Clark Fork River in Montana, unleashing a massive wall of water through the narrow gorge. The enormous wave acted like a bulldozer, gouging out hundreds of thousands of tons of earth and rock as the water rushed to the sea.

Miles and Directions

0.0 Start the hike at the wooden trailhead sign at the south end of the parking lot. Begin walking on a wide, well-graded gravel path beside picturesque Tanner Creek.

0.3 Arrive at a cement fish ladder.

0.4 Cross a footbridge and notice the splashing falls on your left.

0.6 Walk up a flight of wooden steps.

0.8 Come to a fork and go left. (**Option:** The right fork takes you on an optional loop section of the trail.)

0.9 Cross a footbridge.

1.1 Reach the roaring Wahclella Falls (your turnaround point).

2.2 Arrive back at the trailhead.

23 Eagle Creek

This trail through the Columbia River Gorge National Scenic Area leads through a deep, scenic canyon carved by bubbling Eagle Creek and shaded by a canopy of oak, bigleaf maple, and cedar. Along the route, hikers are rewarded with views of half a dozen cascading waterfalls and a creek perfectly suited for a swim during the hot summer months. Backpackers can hike in and camp at any of the four established campsites along the first 7.5 miles of the trail—but note that these sites fill up fast. For more solitude, forge ahead 13.3 miles from the Eagle Creek trailhead to camp at Wahtum Lake.

Distance: 6.4 miles out and back (with longer options)
Approximate hiking time: 2 to 3 hours
Elevation gain: 385 feet
Trail surface: Dirt path; steep drop-offs on some sections of the trail
Best season: Year-round
Other trail users: None
Canine compatibility: Leashed dogs permitted. Use caution with your dog on this trail. There are steep drop-offs; keep your dog leashed at all times.

Fees and permits: Northwest Forest Pass required; passes available by calling (800) 270-7504 or online at www.fs.fed.us/r6/passespermits
Schedule: Open all hours
Maps: USGS: Bonneville Dam, Tanner Butte; Maptech CD: Newport/Portland/Mount Hood/The Dalles
Trail contact: USDA Forest Service, Columbia River Gorge National Scenic Area, 902 Wasco Avenue, Suite 200, Hood River 97031; (541) 308-1700; www.fs.fed.us/r6/columbia

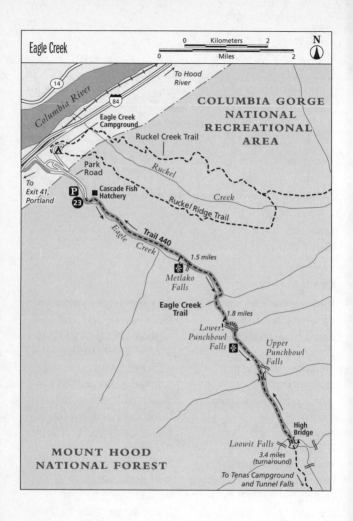

Eagle Creek

0 Kilometers 2
0 Miles 2

N

Columbia River

14
84
To Hood River

Eagle Creek
Campground

Ruckel Creek Trail

**COLUMBIA GORGE
NATIONAL
RECREATIONAL
AREA**

To Exit 41, Portland

Park Road

Ruckel

P
23
Cascade Fish Hatchery

Creek

Ruckel Ridge Trail

Trail 440

Eagle Creek

1.5 miles

Metlako Falls

Eagle Creek Trail

1.8 miles

Lower Punchbowl Falls

Upper Punchbowl Falls

High Bridge

Loowit Falls

3.4 miles (turnaround)

To Tenas Campground and Tunnel Falls

**MOUNT HOOD
NATIONAL FOREST**

Finding the trailhead: From Portland head east on Interstate 84 for about 41 miles. Take exit 41 for Eagle Creek Recreation Area. At the stop sign turn right and stay to the right toward the picnic area and trailhead. Continue about 0.5 mile to a paved parking area at the road's end.

From Hood River head west on I-84 and take exit 40 (Bonneville). Get back on I-84 heading east. Take exit 41 for Eagle Creek Recreation Area. At the stop sign turn right and stay to the right toward the picnic area and trailhead. Continue about 0.5 mile to a paved parking area at the road's end. *DeLorme: Oregon Atlas & Gazetteer:* Page 68 C1

The Hike

Eagle Creek is a classic gorge hike that should not be overlooked by hikers of any level. As you hike this trail, it's hard not to appreciate the time and effort spent creating this engineering marvel that sweeps along the high cliff walls, offering spectacular views of many of the area's different waterfalls. Be forewarned, though, if you're planning on hiking Eagle Creek with children: There are many steep drop-offs along the route, and unsupervised children could be at great risk of falling from one of the trailside cliffs. If you're determined to take your child with you, be sure to keep a close eye on him or her at all times. This same caution applies to dogs. Keep your dog leashed at all times on this trail.

Because of the trail's spectacular scenery and fairly easy grade, this very popular hike is often crowded—especially on sunny summer weekends—so consider making the trip on a weekday to avoid the crowds. Otherwise, be prepared to share this trail with a slew of fellow outdoor enthusiasts.

The trail starts just above the creek and ascends very

slowly over the next 3.4 miles to High Bridge (your turn-around point). Along the route you'll pass twisted oak trees and shady bigleaf maples. In spring and summer, wildflowers along the trail compete with one another in a show of vibrant colors for all who visit to enjoy.

At 0.8 mile there's a section of trail that often proves tricky to those unaccustomed to heights. Fortunately, cables are in place to help hikers navigate this precipitous cliffside stretch of trail. The trail is actually in good shape; it's just the steep drop-off to the right that makes your brain put on the brakes.

After 1.5 miles there's a very short optional side trail to Metlako Falls, which takes its name from the Native American goddess of salmon (in fact, the falls seem to sweep off the basalt cliff like a salmon racing to the sea). At 1.8 miles you'll arrive at the Lower Punchbowl Falls Trail. Descend steeply here for 0.2 mile to the creekbed and falls, a broad cascade that tumbles into a rocky, circular bowl. If it's a hot summer day, this area will be packed with kids, dogs, and others splashing and wading in the water. Walk a short distance upstream to view the tumbling 30-foot cascade of Punchbowl Falls.

As you continue on the Eagle Creek Trail, the gorge becomes steeper and deeper until you reach the High Bridge—a long, skinny expansion bridge that stretches precariously across the canyon. From the middle of the bridge, you'll have a giddy downward view into the deep chasm carved by Eagle Creek. The water rushing through the canyon over mossy boulders and ledges is absolutely mesmerizing.

After the bridge, it's time to turn around and head back the way you came. If you still have some energy left, consider pressing on toward Tenas Campground and Skookni-chuck Falls, 0.4 mile up the trail. Two miles beyond that, you'll arrive at the roaring cascade of Tunnel Falls.

Miles and Directions

0.0 Start hiking on the signed singletrack trail that is lined with oak trees and parallels tumbling Eagle Creek.

0.8 The trail becomes precipitous and drops off steeply to the canyon floor. Watch your footing here!

1.5 Arrive at a side trail on the right that leads to 100-foot Met-lako Falls.

1.8 Turn right onto the Lower Punchbowl Falls Trail.

2.0 Arrive at a viewpoint of 15-foot Lower Punchbowl Falls. Walk along the creek a short distance to view 30-foot Punchbowl Falls. Once you're finished viewing the falls, head back to the main trail.

2.2 Turn right onto the Eagle Creek Trail.

3.4 Arrive at High Bridge—a steel bridge that gives you an amazing view of the narrow creek canyon far below you. This is your turnaround point. Retrace the route back to the trailhead. (**Option:** Continue 0.4 mile to Tenas Campground and Skooknichuck Falls. Two miles beyond Skooknichuck Falls, you'll arrive at the roaring cascade of Tunnel Falls.)

6.4 Arrive back at the trailhead.

24 Historic Columbia River Highway State Trail

Relive the historic past by hiking on a restored section of the Columbia River Highway. On this easy, paved route you'll hike along the edge of the scenic Columbia River Gorge for more than 9 miles on an out-and-back route between Hood River and Mosier. Along the way, you'll be able to stop at many spectacular viewpoints and have the opportunity to pass through the historic Mosier Twin Tunnels.

Distance: 9.2 miles out and back (with a shuttle option)

Approximate hiking time: 2 hours with a shuttle; 4 to 5 hours without a shuttle

Elevation gain: 250 feet

Trail surface: Dirt path

Best season: Year-round

Other trail users: None

Canine compatibility: Leashed dogs permitted

Fees and permits: Park pass, available at self-pay machines at both trailheads

Schedule: Dawn to dusk

Maps: USGS: White Salmon; Maptech CD: Newport/Portland/Mount Hood/The Dalles

Trail contact: Oregon State Parks and Recreation, 725 Summer Street NE, Suite C, Salem 97301; (800) 551-6949; www .oregon.gov/ORPD/PARKS/index .shtml

Finding the trailhead: *Mark O. Hatfield west trailhead in Hood River:* From the intersection of Interstates 205 and 84 in Portland, go 54 miles east on I-84 toward Hood River and The Dalles. Turn off the highway at exit 64 where a sign indicates HOOD RIVER HIGHWAY 35/WHITE SALMON/GOVERNMENT CAMP. At the end of the off-ramp, turn right (south) toward Hood River. Continue 0.3 mile to a stop sign and a four-way intersection. Turn left (east) onto the Old Columbia River Highway. You'll also see a sign indicating HISTORIC STATE PARK TRAIL. Travel 1.3

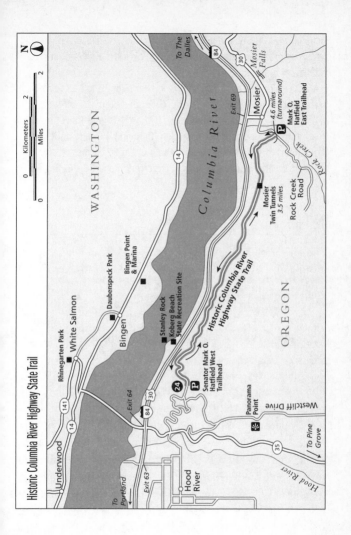

Historic Columbia River Highway State Trail

miles on the Old Columbia River Highway until you reach a parking area, visitor center, and the Mark O. Hatfield west trailhead on the left side of the road.

Mark O. Hatfield east trailhead in Mosier: From Hood River go 5 miles east on I-84 to Mosier (exit 69). At the end of the off-ramp, turn right. Go 0.2 mile and then take a sharp left onto Rock Creek Road at the HISTORIC STATE PARK TRAIL sign. Continue 0.6 mile on Rock Creek Road to the Mark O. Hatfield east trailhead on the left side of the road. *DeLorme: Oregon Atlas & Gazetteer:* Page 68 C4, Page 69 C5

The Hike

The Historic Columbia River State Park Trail takes you on a tour along a historic section of the Columbia River Gorge Highway. This fun, easy route travels for 4.6 miles between the windsurfing capital of Hood River and the small, cozy town of Mosier. This trail is part of the Historic Columbia River Highway that was originally built between 1913 and 1922.

A main feature of this trail is the Mosier Twin Tunnels which were originally designed by Conde B. McCullough, a well-known state bridge engineer for the Oregon Highway Department. The tunnels were built in 1921 and were lined with timbers for extra support and finished with handcrafted stonework. The tunnels also featured viewing portals and a mesmerizing cliff walk that was built right into the cliff outside the tunnels. In addition to the Mosier Twin Tunnels, two other tunnels, Oneonta and Mitchell Point, were built along the Historic Columbia River Highway between 1914 and 1921. When the original highway was relocated in the 1950s, the tunnels were filled with rock and abandoned.

In May 2000, Secretary of the Interior Bruce Babbitt announced that 51 of the original 55 miles of the Historic Columbia River Highway between Troutdale and The Dalles had been designated a National Historic Landmark. An employee of the Oregon Department of Transportation, Robert W. Hadlow, Ph.D., nominated the Historic Columbia River Highway for this special designation, writing: "It is an outstanding example of modern highway development in twentieth-century America for its pioneering advances in road design. The road, and its associated designed landscape, was a technical and civic achievement of its time, successfully mixing ambitious engineering with sensitivity to the magnificent landscape."

The Mosier Twin Tunnels section of the highway is one of many sites that have been restored and reopened for the public to enjoy. This spectacular 4.6-mile section of trail was opened in July 2000 and cost a hefty $5.6 million! A large percentage of the project was funded with federal dollars, and the remainder was paid for with private donations.

Why did it cost so much? Rock fall at the west tunnel entrance had always been a danger, and it was up to the Oregon Department of Transportation to come up with a viable solution. The solution they chose is a concrete deck structure made up of foam and cement that rests on concrete pillars. The concrete structure is anchored to the cliff with 25-foot anchor bars. This structure is designed to support the impact of a 5,000-pound rock falling from a height of 200 feet. To be sure the structure blended into the natural surroundings, the concrete was tinted a very dark gray to blend in with the surrounding basalt cliff. This amazing project took five years to complete—you will understand why when you ride under the concrete deck and explore the inside of the tunnels.

Before starting your hike, be sure to stop at the visitor center and check out the interpretive displays describing the restoration process of this historic route. The friendly folks staffing the desk inside can fill your head with dozens of other things to see and do while you are in the area.

Miles and Directions

0.0 Start hiking east on the paved trail adjacent to the visitor center where a trail sign indicates SENATOR MARK O. HATFIELD WEST TRAILHEAD. (FYI: On the first part of the route, you'll walk through a wetter ecosystem of fir trees mixed with bigleaf maple and other deciduous tree species. In spring, bright purple lupine and bright yellow balsamroot add splashes of color next to the trail.)

0.2 Pass an interpretive sign on your right that describes the different ecosystems along the route.

2.7 Pass a viewpoint on your left of the Columbia River and cliff-lined gorge.

3.5 Enter the Mosier Twin Tunnels. (FYI: From inside the tunnels you'll have opportunities to stop and soak in more stunning views of the gorge.)

3.7 Exit the Mosier Twin Tunnels.

3.8 Pass a side trail on the left leading to a viewpoint where you may catch glimpses to the north (on a clear day) of Mount St. Helens and Mount Adams.

4.4 At the T-intersection and stop sign, turn right and head uphill to the Mark O. Hatfield east trailhead.

4.6 Arrive at the Mark O. Hatfield east trailhead and your turnaround point (or your ending point if you left a shuttle vehicle at this trailhead). (FYI: This trailhead also has water, restrooms, and a phone.)

9.2 Arrive back at the trailhead.

25 Deschutes River State Park Trail

This route follows the shores of the swift-running Deschutes River in Deschutes River State Park and then hooks up with the doubletrack rail trail that takes you back to your starting point. The hike offers great views of the river and a chance to view a variety of wildlife present in the sagebrush-scented Deschutes River Canyon. There is also an overnight campground in this state park if you want to stay for a few days.

Distance: 3.7-mile loop (with longer options)

Approximate hiking time: 1.5 to 2 hours

Elevation gain: 75 feet

Trail surface: Dirt path, doubletrack road

Best season: Year-round

Other trail users: Mountain bikers, equestrians

Canine compatibility: Leashed dogs permitted

Fees and permits: Parking pass required

Schedule: Dawn to dusk

Maps: USGS: Emerson, Wishram; Maptech CD: Newport/Portland/Mount Hood/The Dalles; Deschutes River State Park Trail map available by contacting Oregon State Parks (800-551-6949; www.oregonstateparks.org/park_37.php)

Trail contact: Oregon State Parks and Recreation, 725 Summer Street NE, Suite C, Salem 97301; (800) 551-6949; www.oregon.gov/ORPD/PARKS/index.shtml

Finding the trailhead: From The Dalles travel 14 miles east on Interstate 84 to exit 97 for HIGHWAY 206/CELILO PARK/DESCHUTES RIVER STATE PARK. Turn right at the end of the off-ramp and then take an immediate left onto Highway 206. Head east for 3.1 miles and turn right into the entrance for Deschutes River State Park. Proceed 0.4 mile on the paved road through the campground to where it dead-ends at the trailhead sign. *DeLorme: Oregon Atlas & Gazetteer:* Page 84 B1

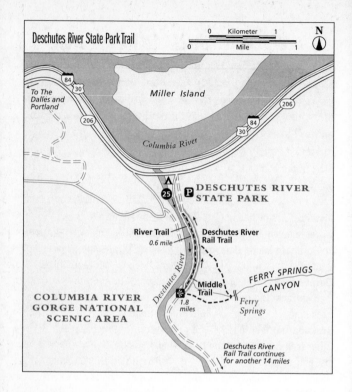

Deschutes River State Park Trail

Miller Island

Columbia River

To The
Dalles and
Portland

DESCHUTES RIVER
STATE PARK

River Trail
0.6 mile

Deschutes River
Rail Trail

FERRY SPRINGS
CANYON

Middle
Trail
1.8
miles

Ferry
Springs

COLUMBIA RIVER
GORGE NATIONAL
SCENIC AREA

Deschutes River
Rail Trail continues
for another 14 miles

The Hike

This short loop trail begins in Deschutes River State Park and travels through the scenic Deschutes River Canyon, a prodigious chasm averaging more than 2,000 feet deep and filled with interesting geological history. Forty million years ago this canyon was part of a flat, semitropical plain suspected of receiving more than 240 inches of rain per year. Thirty million years ago the Continental Plate collided with the Pacific Plate, lifting the land upward to form the Coastal and Cascade Mountain Ranges. This cataclysmic event caused the earth's crust to fracture and hot molten magma to rise to the surface, creating gigantic basalt flows. As you hike through this deep canyon, steep, eroding basalt walls speak their own stories. Curved layers bend and push against one another creating bulges, breaks, and unique columns, carrying one's imagination millions of years into the past.

The high walls of the river canyon provide excellent habitat for red-tailed hawks and other birds of prey, and the Deschutes River attracts plenty of ospreys and blue herons. The river's abundant aquatic vegetation and grassy banks also attract Canada geese, mallard ducks, and a variety of other waterfowl.

You'll follow the River Trail for 1.4 miles along the shores of the fast-flowing Deschutes River. Then you'll turn left and climb up a steep, rocky trail to a dramatic viewpoint of Rattlesnake Rapids. From here you have the option of returning to your starting point or tackling a longer hike by turning right on the Deschutes River multiuse trail, which travels 14 more miles up the canyon. If you want to stay and explore this area for a few days, you can set up camp at the Deschutes River State Park campground.

Miles and Directions

0.0 Start hiking across a large grassy field paralleling the scenic Deschutes River.

0.1 Arrive at a wooden trail sign indicating that the River Trail is to the right and the Middle and Upper Trails are to the left. Go right and begin hiking on the smooth singletrack of the River Trail.

0.6 Continue straight (right) on the River Trail. (The Middle Trail goes left at this intersection.)

0.7 Cross several wooden ramps over a marshy area.

1.2 Cross a small spring-fed creek.

1.4 Turn left toward Upper Trail/Middle Trail. Power up a steep hill over a rough, rocky section of the trail.

1.8 Arrive at a scenic overlook of Rattlesnake Rapids and an interpretive sign. The trail swings left and then down a short, rocky section for about 50 yards to a doubletrack road. Turn left onto the doubletrack road. (**Option:** If you are still feeling energetic, turn right and follow the doubletrack road for 14.0 more miles as it follows the course of the Deschutes River.)

3.5 Turn left onto a singletrack trail that takes you on a steep descent toward the river.

3.6 Turn right into the wide, grassy field and continue 0.1 mile back to the trailhead.

3.7 Arrive back at the trailhead.

26 Lost Lake Loop

This easy 3.0-mile route takes you on a tour around picturesque Lost Lake in Mount Hood National Forest. Perks include spectacular views of Mount Hood, pockets of old-growth forest, and opportunities for swimming.

Distance: 3.0-mile loop
Approximate hiking time: 1 hour
Elevation gain: None
Trail surface: Dirt path
Best season: June through October
Other trail users: None
Canine compatibility: Leashed dogs permitted
Fees and permits: Northwest Forest Pass required; passes available by calling (800) 270-7504 or online at www.fs .fed.us/r6/passespermits
Schedule: Open all hours
Maps: USGS: Bull Run Lake; Maptech CD: Newport/Portland/ Mount Hood/The Dalles
Trail contact: Mount Hood National Forest Headquarters Office, 16400 Champion Way, Sandy 97055; (503) 668-1700; www.fs.fed.us/r6/mthood

Finding the trailhead: From the intersection of Interstates 205 and 84 in Portland, head east 7.2 miles on I-84 to exit 13 for 238th Drive/Wood Village. Turn right onto 238th Drive and proceed 2.9 miles. Turn left onto Burnside Road. Travel 1 mile and then turn left (east) onto U.S. Highway 26. Continue 27.5 miles east on US 26 to the town of Zigzag. At the Zigzag Store turn left (north) onto East Lolo Pass Road. Travel 10.9 miles on East Lolo Pass Road to the intersection with unsigned gravel Forest Road 1810 (McKee Creek Road), which is the first right turn after signed Forest Road 828. Turn right on FR 1810 and continue 7.5 miles until the road intersects Forest Road 18. Proceed 7 miles on pavement to the intersection with Forest Road 13. Turn left onto FR 13 and travel 6 miles to the pay booth at Lost Lake. After the entry booth, stay right as the road

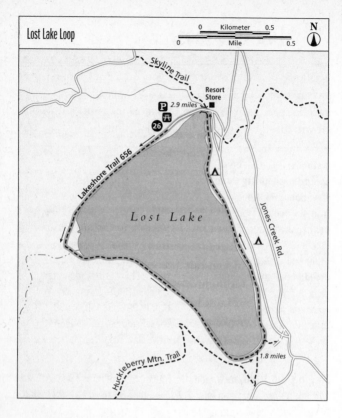

Lost Lake Loop

0   Kilometer   0.5
0   Mile   0.5

N

Skyline Trail

Resort Store

P 2.9 miles

26

Lakeshore Trail 656

Lost Lake

Jones Creek Rd.

Huckleberry Mtn. Trail

1.8 miles

parallels the lake. Continue past the general store to the road's end at a day-use picnic area.

From I-84 in Hood River, take exit 62, signed WEST HOOD RIVER. Travel about 1 mile into Hood River and take a right onto Thirteenth Street. Travel approximately 3.5 miles to Odell. Cross a bridge and turn right past Tucker Park and travel 6.3 miles. Stay right toward Dee. From the small town of Dee, travel 14 miles, following signs to Lost Lake. After the pay booth at the lake, stay right as the road parallels the lake. Continue past the general store to the road's end at a day-use picnic area. *DeLorme: Oregon Atlas & Gazetteer:* Page 62 A2

The Hike

You'll begin hiking on this route in a counterclockwise direction on Lakeshore Trail 656. The path is wide, smooth, and fast and travels beneath a shady forest canopy of cedar and hemlock trees. Looking across the lake, you'll have a picturesque view of Mount Hood. You'll follow this path as it circles a quick 3.0 miles around the lake. If you want to explore this area further, you can stay at the campground. If you're looking for more comfortable accommodations, Lost Lake Resort (541-386-6366) rents cabins that are located right on the lake.

Miles and Directions

0.0   From the parking area begin hiking counterclockwise around the lake on Lakeshore Trail 656. (FYI: Make a note of the intersection where the parking lot access trail meets the Lakeshore Trail. This will be your exit trail after you finish the lake loop.)

0.6   Cross a boardwalk that travels through a marshy area filled with skunk cabbage and marsh grasses.

1.8   Arrive at a trail intersection with the signed Huckleberry Mountain Trail. Stay to the left and continue on the Lakeshore Trail. Continue another 100 yards to another trail junction where a sign indicates TO OLD GROWTH TRAIL/GROUP CAMP/DAY USE AREA 1 MILE. Veer left.

2.5   The trail becomes pavement.

2.8   The paved path intersects a paved road at an unsigned junction. Veer left and continue hiking on a gravel path.

2.9   Cross a footbridge over Lake Branch Creek.

3.0   Turn right and walk up a short set of stairs to arrive back at the parking area and your starting point.

27 Mirror Lake Loop

This trail has everything you ever wanted: a smooth trail; a bubbling creek and scenic alpine lake; a spectacular view of Mount Hood; wildflowers; and cool, shady forest. If it sounds too good to be true, there is a catch—this trail is very popular and very crowded (especially on summer weekends). If you can look past the crowds, you'll love the hike to this high alpine lake that offers prime swimming opportunities in midsummer.

Distance: 3.2-mile lollipop
Approximate hiking time: 1.5 to 2.5 hours
Elevation gain: 605 feet
Trail surface: Dirt path
Best season: June through October
Other trail users: None
Canine compatibility: Leashed dogs permitted
Fees and permits: Northwest Forest Pass required; passes available by calling (800) 270-7504 or online at www.fs.fed.us/r6/passespermits
Schedule: Open all hours
Maps: USGS: Government Camp; Maptech CD: Newport/Portland/Mount Hood/The Dalles
Trail contact: Mount Hood National Forest Headquarters Office, 16400 Champion Way, Sandy 97055; (503) 668-1700; www.fs.fed.us/r6/mthood

Finding the trailhead: From the intersection of Interstates 205 and 84 in Portland, head east for 7.2 miles on I-84 to exit 13 for 238th Drive/Wood Village. Turn right onto 238th Drive and proceed 2.9 miles. Turn left onto Burnside Road. Continue about 1 mile and turn left (east) onto U.S. Highway 26. Travel east on US 26 to an unmarked trailhead between Mileposts 51 and 52 on the right (south) side of the highway.

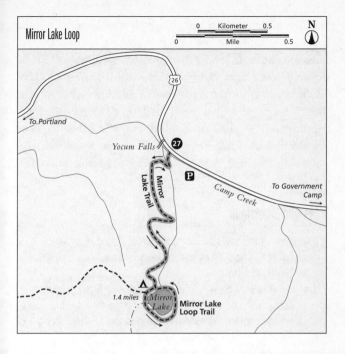

0   Kilometer   0.5

0   Mile   0.5

N

26

To Portland

Yocum Falls

27

Mirror Lake Trail

P

Camp Creek

To Government Camp

1.4 miles

Mirror Lake

Mirror Lake Loop Trail

From Hood River head south on Highway 35 to the junction with US 26. Turn right (west) onto US 26 and travel west to Government Camp. From Government Camp continue approximately 2 miles west on US 26 to an unmarked trailhead on the left (south) side of the highway between Mileposts 51 and 52. *DeLorme: Oregon Atlas & Gazetteer*: Page 62 B2

The Hike

This route takes you on a tour of beautiful Mirror Lake in Mount Hood National Forest. You'll begin the hike by ascending a series of switchbacks through a cool, shady forest. After 1.4 miles you'll begin the loop portion of the hike along the shores of picturesque Mirror Lake. This high lake trail is decorated with deep purple lupine, vibrant red Indian paintbrush, and other colorful wildflowers. From this trail you'll have stunning views of Mount Hood. Also be on the lookout for some nice swimming holes. After a short 0.4-mile trek, you'll end the loop portion of the hike and descend 1.4 miles back to the trailhead. This is a very popular trail and can be crowded on summer weekends. To avoid the crowds, hike the trail on a weekday or in the fall months.

Miles and Directions

0.0 Start at the trailhead on US 26. Cross a footbridge across bubbling Camp Creek and hook up with the smooth, wide Mirror Lake Trail.

1.4 Arrive at a T-intersection and the beginning of the signed Mirror Lake Loop Trail. Turn right and circle the lake in a counterclockwise direction. At the next trail junction, stay to the left and continue on the loop around the lake.

1.8 End the loop portion of the route. Turn right and head downhill on the same route back to your starting point.

3.2 Arrive back at the trailhead.

28 Salmon River

Mount Hood National Forest's Salmon River Trail takes hikers on a journey through a mossy old-growth forest next to the Salmon River, a designated Wild and Scenic River. The trail begins by hugging the edge of the Salmon River. It then climbs a steep ridge, ending with a short loop that offers impressive views of Salmon River Canyon and the surrounding forested ridges of the Salmon-Huckleberry Wilderness.

Distance: 7.2 miles out and back

Approximate hiking time: 3 to 4 hours

Elevation gain: 950 feet

Trail surface: Dirt path

Best season: June through October

Other trail users: None

Canine compatibility: Leashed dogs permitted

Fees and permits: Northwest Forest Pass required; passes available by calling (800) 270-7504 or online at www.fs.fed.us/r6/passespermits

Schedule: Open all hours

Maps: USGS: Rhododendron; Maptech CD: Newport/Portland/Mount Hood/The Dalles

Trail contact: Zigzag Ranger Station, 70220 East U.S. Highway 26, Zigzag 97049; (503) 622-3191; www.fs.fed.us/r6/mthood

Finding the trailhead: From Portland travel 42 miles east on U.S. Highway 26 to Zigzag. Turn right (south) onto Salmon River Road and travel 4.9 miles to the parking area and trailhead on the left side of the road. *DeLorme: Oregon Atlas & Gazetteer:* Page 62 B1

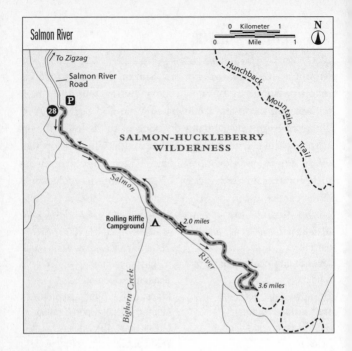

To Zigzag

Salmon River
Road

P

28

SALMON-HUCKLEBERRY
WILDERNESS

Salmon

Rolling Riffle
Campground   ▲   2.0 miles

River

3.6 miles

Hunchback

Mountain Trail

Bighorn Creek

The Hike

Salmon River Trail 742 traipses through the 44,560-acre Salmon-Huckleberry Wilderness, which was established in 1984. Located about an hour from the Portland metropolitan area, the Salmon River has carved a splendid canyon with prominent ridges, buttes, and pinnacles. Chinook and coho salmon spawn in its clear waters, and anglers enjoy casting for steelhead trout in its rushing currents.

Major landmarks in the Salmon-Huckleberry include Huckleberry Mountain to the north, 5,045-foot Devils Peak to the east, and 4,877-foot Salmon Butte to the south. As its name implies, the wilderness is well known for its purplish, pea-size huckleberries, most abundant near Devils Peak and Huckleberry Mountain. The enticing blue fruit, related to blueberries, is usually ripe by late August and makes for a delicious treat if you happen across some while out along the trail.

The Salmon River trailhead is 4.9 miles south of Zigzag off Salmon River Road (Forest Road 2618). Large red alders, Douglas firs, and western hemlocks shade the trail, and towering old-growth trees give the forest a mystical quality. Beneath these giants are the broad, fan-shaped leaves of vine maple and thick bunches of raspberry bushes. Wildlife includes black bear, mule deer, cougar, badger, and marten.

The trail begins by paralleling the shallow, boulder-strewn Salmon River, which carves its way westward and eventually empties into the Sandy River near Brightwood, 4 miles west of Zigzag off US 26. The river, which flows for a total of 31 miles, receives its water as snowmelt from Mount Hood's Palmer Glacier. At 0.4 mile you'll pass a cliff where thick stems of Oregon stonecrop have a firm grasp on the rocky ledges. The bright yellow flowers of this hardy plant thrive in the sunshine that basks the cliff walls.

At 1.5 miles you'll come to Rolling Riffle Campground, and after 2 miles you'll cross a footbridge and enter the Salmon-Huckleberry Wilderness. The trail climbs a steep ridge at the base of Devils Peak for the next 1.5 miles. At the top of the ridge is an unsigned trail junction. Take a right and walk a short distance to a spectacular view of the canyon and the river far below.

From here the trail makes a loop along the edge of the ridge. When you've finished the loop, return the way you came.

Miles and Directions

0.0 Start on the singletrack trail located on the far end of the parking area next to the bridge. The trail takes you close to the river through big old-growth cedars and Douglas fir trees.

2.0 Cross a footbridge and arrive at a self-issue wilderness permit station. Fill out a wilderness permit and then continue your journey.

3.4 Turn right to begin a short loop.

3.5 You'll exit the trees onto a grassy ridge with spectacular views of the river canyon. (Note: Watch your footing on the trail—it can be loose and slippery.)

3.6 Turn left at a T-junction.

3.8 The loop section of the trail ends. Veer right and retrace the route back to the trailhead.

7.2 Arrive back at the trailhead.

Acknowledgments

Thanks to Ken Skeen for his editorial advice; to Bear, my canine hiking companion; and to Paulette Baker for editing the manuscript.

About the Author

Lizann Dunegan is a freelance writer and photographer who specializes in writing outdoor guidebooks and travel articles about the Northwest. Her other books include *Canine Oregon, Best Easy Day Hikes North Oregon Coast, Hiking the Oregon Coast, Hiking Oregon, Mountain Biking Oregon, Road Riding Oregon, Trail Running Oregon,* and *Insiders' Guide to the Oregon Coast.*

Lizann enjoys exploring the trails in Oregon with her partner, Ken Skeen; her dog, Bear; and her Andalusian horse, Miguel. Lizann also enjoys trail running, cycling, and spinning and knitting wool.